The Truth About Mormonism

THE TRUTH ABOUT MORMONISM

A Former Adherent Analyzes the LDS Faith

Weldon Langfield

Weldon Langfield Publications
Bakersfield, California

Weldon Langfield Publications
4450 California Ave., Suite 137
Bakersfield, CA 93309

To Vicki

Contents

Preface

Jesus said, "If any man is willing to do his will he shall know of the doctrine, whether it be of God, or whether I speak of myself" (John 7:17). Christ's doctrine is the New Testament, so the Bible there teaches that anyone deeply wanting to obey God will be able to ascertain the truth. Paul expressed a similar sentiment in Ephesians 3:4 when he wrote, "Whereby, when ye read ye may understand my knowledge in the mystery of Christ."

Having been raised in and baptized in the Reorganized Church of Jesus Christ of Latter Day Saints, my earliest memories, religiously speaking, are of attending services of that fellowship in California, first in Monterey and later in Bakersfield. While in college in Fresno I began attending the RLDS church, as it is also known, on Sunday mornings while visiting evening services of the Church of Christ. The more I was exposed to the Bible, the more difficulties I had with the *Book of Mormon* and "The Prophet" Joseph Smith. There seemed to be no one at the RLDS congregation who could or would answer my questions logically. It was at this time that I found the truth was in the Bible and became a Christian.

This book is written without any animosity or sense of vindictiveness. It is hoped that this volume will enable non-Mormons to get enough of a feel for the Mormon faith to protect themselves from the influence of the Latter-day Saint doctrine. Perhaps some Mormons, through the influence of this book, will take an objective look at their faith. This volume does not claim to be an exhaustive treatment of the subject. Rather, it represents an attempt to present the fruit of decades of interest and study in the most concise and convincing manner possible.

The first four chapters of this book, "Early Mormonism," "The Book of Mormon," "Doctrines of Mormonism," and "Smith's Other Works" are intended to give the reader exposure to many of the serious problems in Mormonism. In these chapters, LDS writings have been consulted and documented. The greatest difficulty I had in developing a solid Christian faith was overcoming years of teaching that the Bible was inaccurate, inadequate and insufficient. I believe that to be an often overlooked but extremely common problem of followers of Joseph Smith, Jr., since it can be safely said that the lack of trustworthiness of the Bible is a fundamental doctrine of Mormonism. That is why, in my opinion, Mormons, when persuaded of the untruthfulness of their faith, often fail to convert to Christianity and instead completely reject religion. For that reason, the last chapter, "Can the Bible be Trusted?" presents evidence of the integrity of the Scriptures.

The Church of Jesus Christ of Latter-day Saints, headquartered in Salt Lake City, Utah, is the largest body of those who consider Joseph Smith, Jr. to be a prophet. Because that group uses the King James Version of the Bible (also known as the Authorized Version), all scripture quotations are taken from it.

Chapter 1

Early Mormonism

The United States of America is, to a large extent, the product of the quest for religious freedom. Quakers, Congregationalists, Baptists and many others came to the New World seeking a more favorable climate in which to practice their convictions. It should not be surprising that a nation spawned by religious impetus should itself beget religious movements. Indeed it has. The Shakers, Jehovah's Witnesses, Seventh-Day Adventists, and the Apostolic movement are a few of the religions which have their roots in the American frontier. Of the groups which germinated in the fertile religious soil of North America, none has had a more colorful history than the Church of Jesus Christ of Latter-day Saints.

Joseph Smith, Jr., the founder, was born on December 23, 1805, in Sharon, Vermont, to Joseph and Lucy Mack Smith. In 1817, when Smith was eleven years old, his family settled near Palmyra, New York, not far from present-day Rochester. Within a few years, most of the Smith family had become Presbyterians. Since Mormonism cannot be separated from Joseph Smith, Jr., it is at this point that Latter-day Saint literature usually begins to tell the story of the origin of the religion.

The Mormon Account of Their Origin

Unlike other family members, Joseph couldn't decide which church to join. In 1820, Smith, when in his fifteenth year, became deeply troubled about the religious division that surrounded him. His attention was drawn to the disunity because of a great revival which took place in the area. Smith would later comment, as recorded in a section of *Pearl of Great Price* known as Joseph Smith 2:

> Some time in the second year after our removal to Manchester, there was in the place where we lived an unusual excitement on the subject of religion. It commenced with the Methodists, but soon became general among all sects in that region of country, indeed the whole district of our country seemed affected by it, and great multitudes united themselves to the different religious parties which created no small stir and divisions amongst the people, some crying, "Lo, here!" and others, "Lo, there!" Some were contending for the Methodist faith, some for the Presbyterian, and some for the Baptist....During this time of great excitement my mind was called up to serious reflection...So, in accordance with this, my determination to ask of God, I retired to the woods to make the attempt.[1]

Motivated, then, by great uneasiness over competition between various churches, he prayed to know which denomination was the true one. Smith was moved to petition God by the Bible teaching of James 1:5: "If any of you lack wisdom, let him ask of God that giveth to all men liberally, and upbraideth not; and it shall be given him." As young Joseph prayed, a pillar of light appeared overhead with two personages. One pointed to the other, saying, "This is my beloved Son, Hear him." The awe-struck youth afterward told a Methodist minister of this vision. Smith later wrote, "He treated my communication not only lightly but with such great contempt, saying it was all of the devil."[2]

About three years later, while praying for forgiveness of sins, Joseph Smith had a second vision, in which an angel named Moroni appeared three successive times. Moroni said that God had an important work for him to do. The angel told Smith that his name "should be had for good and evil among all nations, kindreds and tongues." In the vision Moroni revealed to him the existence of golden plates on which the history of former inhabitants of the American continents were engraved. These plates, Smith was assured, contained "the fullness of the everlasting gospel."

Additionally revealed to Smith was the existence of two stones, fastened to a breastplate, called the Urim and Thummim, which was with the golden plates. The Urim and Thummim was a God-given device for miraculously translating the language on the plates into English. During the vision, Moroni quoted some Old Testament scriptures differently from the way they're found in the Bible, suggesting the passages are not accurately rendered.

The next day, Smith had yet another vision in which the same angel appeared to him while working. Moroni repeated the previous message, this time including directions to the golden plates. Smith obtained his father's permission to leave work and went to the place where the angel had indicated the plates were located. He found them in a stone box, along with the Urim and Thummim and the breastplate, just as the angel had said. When Smith tried to take the objects out of the box, he was forbidden by the messenger, and was told the time for revealing them was yet four years off. Smith went back to the same location each year, only to see the same angel and receive further information about God's plans.[3]

Finally, on September 22, 1827, Joseph Smith, Jr. was permitted to dig up the ancient records on the Hill Cumorah in New York state. Because of persecution which followed the discovery of the plates, he moved to his father-in-law's home in Harmony Township, Pennsylvania. There Smith found not only refuge from his persecutors, but also a peaceful place to translate the plates. While in Pennsylvania, Martin Harris, a successful farmer, visited him. Harris was favorably impressed with Smith's work and assisted in the task of translating the records. By June 14, 1828, Joseph had dictated to Harris 116 pages of the *Book of Mormon.*

In an effort to convince his wife of the genuineness of the "new revelation," Harris obtained Smith's permission to take the pages home. While with Harris, they disappeared. That portion of the manuscript was not retranslated. Joseph Smith's claimed reason for not again translating those pages was that his enemies could alter the original and belittle him.

From that point, Smith was assisted by Oliver Cowdery.[4] Cowdery never saw the plates; a curtain separated him from Smith. He simply recorded the translation as Joseph Smith dictated it. The *Book of Mormon* was printed by Egbert B. Grandin of Palmyra, New York, with the $5,000 cost financed by Martin Harris. On March 26, 1830, the completed volume went on sale in a Palmyra, New York, bookstore.[5] Within two weeks at Fayette, New York, the "Church of Christ," as the Mormons originally called themselves, was officially organized.

Discrepancies in the Mormon Account

The Mormon account of the beginning of the religion is riddled with discrepancies and problems. In the first place, there was no revival in the Palmyra area in 1820 when Smith claimed to have received his first revelation. Extensive research of church records and newspaper accounts by Protestant minister Wesley P. Walters indicates that a revival did not take place until 1824 when Joseph was nearly nineteen years old. The records of the three churches mentioned by Smith indicate that 1820 was a completely sterile year. The Presbyterians reported no revivals, the Baptists reported a gain of only six members, and the Methodist church showed a loss of six members in the district.[6]

It is apparent, then, that the Mormon account of its origin begins with a gross fabrication. The significance of the finding that the LDS church was launched by a lie cannot be overstated. Mormon missionaries frequently begin their presentations with an account of the first vision, and Mormon tracts and literature emphasize it. Page thirteen of a vividly illustrated Mormon tract titled *Apostasy and Restoration* says, "In 1820, the Lord appeared personally to the prophet Joseph Smith, through whom the true church has been restored."[7] If true, Smith's account would be pivotal in establishing the veracity of Mormonism. Yet the very circumstance that Smith claims led him into the woods to pray, competition between denominations in his area, did not even exist.

Second, Joseph Smith, Jr. is the only witness to the visions which launched the Mormon religion. In other words, the entire foundation of the Church of Jesus Christ of Latter-day Saints is built upon the testimony of one teenage boy. This, of course, directly contradicts the Bible which commands in Matthew 18:16, "In the mouth of two or three witnesses every word may be established." There is a stark, dramatic contrast between the supposed eyewitness evidence of the miraculous beginning of Mormonism and the evidence for the miraculous basis of Christianity, the resurrection of Christ. Paul wrote in 1 Corinthians 15:3-8:

> For I delivered unto you first of all that which I also received, how that Christ died for our sins according to the scriptures; and that he was buried, and that he rose again the third day according to the scriptures: and that he was seen of Cephas, then of the twelve: after that, he was seen of above five hundred brethren at once; of whom the greater part remain unto this present, but some are fallen asleep. After that, he was seen of James; then of all the

apostles. And last of all he was seen of me also, as of one born out of due time.

God, unlike the Mormon church, doesn't expect people to embrace the Christian faith on the basis of a claim made by one or even a few adherents. Literally hundreds saw and testified that Christ was raised from the dead.

Third, when Joseph Smith, Jr. prayed the first time, seeking insight into which church to join, he claimed to be motivated by James 1:5, which says, "If any of you lack wisdom, let him ask of God that giveth to all men liberally, and upbraideth not; and it shall be given him." James 1:5 teaches Christians to pray for wisdom. Smith, however, was praying for knowledge. For knowledge he should have studied the Bible. Jesus taught that truth can be known when he said, "Ye shall know the truth and the truth shall make you free" (John 8:32). In John 17:17, Jesus taught where truth can be found when he said, "Thy word is truth." Knowledge of the truth can be attained, then, by carefully studying the Word of God.

The Bible is fully equipped to give us insight into all matters of faith and practice, including the proper church. We read in 2 Tim. 3:16-17, "All scripture is given by inspiration of God, and is profitable for reproof, for correction, for instruction in righteousness: that the man of God may be perfect, thoroughly furnished unto all good works."

Fourth, when Smith prayed to God, he said he was told to hear God's Son. Unfortunately, he refused to do that. If he had wanted to listen to the Son of God, he should have studied and accepted the authority of the Bible, in which Jesus spoke to all in the "latter days." Hebrews 1:1-2 says, "God, who at sundry times and in divers manners spake in time past unto the fathers by the prophets, hath in these last days spoken unto us by his Son, whom he hath appointed heir of all things, by whom also he made the worlds."

The New Testament, which is centered in Jesus Christ, is the last word from God. In it, Christ warned about false teachers. In Matthew 7:15 Jesus said, "Beware of false prophets, which come to you in sheep's clothing, but inwardly they are ravening wolves." He also indicated that his inspired followers would continue to teach the truth after he left earth. Christ said, "But the Comforter, which is the Holy Ghost, whom the Father will send in my name, he shall teach you all things, and bring all things to your remembrance, whatsoever I have said unto you" (John 14:26). Jesus further declared, "Howbeit when he, the Spirit of truth, is come, he will guide you into all truth" (John 16:13).

Among the verities revealed by Christ's inspired followers is the fact that there was but one delivery of the faith to mankind. In Jude 3, the Bible says to "earnestly contend for the faith which was once delivered unto the saints." By the time Jude wrote, the faith had been "delivered." That leaves no room for a *Book of Mormon* or any other "inspired" document after the close of the New Testament era.

Finally, if an angel did speak to Smith, and this author doesn't believe for a moment he did, that still would not prove the truth of the LDS faith. The apostle Paul taught in 2 Corinthians 11:14, "For Satan himself is transformed into an angel of light." The angel seen by Smith could have been the devil in disguise. Even if it were granted that a real angel actually appeared to Smith, that would merely mean that both the angel and Joseph Smith stand condemned. The Bible says in Galatians 1:8-9, "But though we, or an angel from heaven, preach any other gospel unto you than that which we have preached unto you, let him be accursed. As we said before, so say I now again, If any man preach any other gospel unto you than that ye have received, let him be accursed." The angel stands condemned for preaching another gospel. Smith stands condemned for believing him.

These blatant discrepancies are enough to destroy Mormonism. Clearly, the "tree" of the LDS religion has no roots.

Smith's Character

Mormonism and Joseph Smith, Jr. are inseparable. He is the heart and soul of the religion. The LDS faith is based on his account of some purported visions, and the entire religion stands or falls with him. Joseph Fielding Smith, a noted LDS historian, observed of Joseph:

> He was either a prophet of God, divinely called, properly appointed and commissioned, or he was one of the biggest frauds this world has seen. There is no middle ground. If Joseph Smith was a deceiver, who willfully attempted to mislead the people, then he should be exposed; his claims should be refuted and his doctrines should be shown to be false.[8]

Before me is a training book for Mormon missionaries, *Truth Restored*, which asserts on the first page, "Joseph and Lucy Mack Smith and their eight children...were a typical New England family." Nothing could be further from the truth. Quite to the contrary, Smith came from a family of "ne'er do wells." His father was a poor, mystical treasure hunter who spent much time searching for Captain Kidd's treasure which he imagined was hidden in the ground on the Smith property. When his fortune hunting efforts didn't pan out, the senior Smith even attempted to mint his own money. Judge Daniel Woodward, a former neighbor, said in *Historical Magazine* in 1870, "He also became implicated with one Jack Downing in counterfeiting money, but turned state's evidence and escaped the penalty."[9]

Joseph's mother was known for her religious gullibility and superstitious nature. One historian wrote, "Lucy Smith had neither the education nor natural intelligence as would interfere with such 'beliefs' as came to her from family tradition, from her own literal interpretation of the Bible, or from the workings of her imagination." Mrs. Smith had seen visions, experienced miraculous healing, and, by a prayer in a grove, supposedly effected the supernatural cure of her daughter.[10]

Joseph Smith, Jr., after his first vision, was apparently not greatly influenced. With his father, he continued to dig for Captain Kidd's treasure. Smith later denied engaging in money digging, as the pastime was then called, but documentation overwhelmingly proves that he did. In the course of searching for hidden gold he used "peep stones"—rocks which he imagined he could place in the crown of his hat and, holding the hat to his face, "see" where riches were concealed.

Smith even hired out as a treasure hunter. In fact, he was tried in the case of *State of New York v. Joseph Smith*. In the trial, he was accused of being a disorderly person and an impostor, claiming to find buried treasure by looking into stones. Judge Albert Neely's bill for costs called the case the trial of "Joseph Smith the glass looker." Smith was found guilty.[11] All of these events took place in the year 1826. Mormon chronology places the trial after several years of magnificent visions in which God, Christ, John the Baptist, and angels periodically spoke to him. The trial was only a year before the golden plates were allegedly entrusted to Smith.[12]

Shortly after the Mormon church was established, opponents began to accumulate evidence of the true character of its founder. Pomeroy Tucker, writing in *The Origin, Rise and Progress of Mormonism* in 1867, collected numerous sworn statements from Smith's family and neighbors. The unanimous testimony was that Smith was known for "his habits of exaggeration and untruthfulness...his word was received with the least confidence by those who knew him best."[13] E.D. Howe, a contemporary of Joseph Smith, produced a statement signed by sixty-two residents of Palmyra, New York. It read:

We the undersigned, have been acquainted with the Smith family, for a number of years, while they resided near this place, and we have no hesitation in saying, that we consider them destitute of that moral character, which ought to entitle them to the confidence of any community. They were particularly famous for visionary projects, spent much of their time in diggings for money which they pretended was hid in the earth; and to this day, large excavations may be seen in the earth, not far from their residence, where they used to spend their time in digging for hidden treasures. Joseph Smith, Sr., and his son Joseph, were in particular, considered entirely destitute of moral character, and addicted to vicious habits.[14]

Isaac Hale, Joseph Smith's father-in-law, described the young "prophet" in the following excerpt from a lengthy affidavit:

I first became acquainted with Joseph Smith, Jr. in November 25, 1825. He was at that time in the employ of a set of men who were called "money diggers," and his occupation was that of seeing, or pretending to see by means of a stone placed in his hat, and his hat closed over his face. His appearance at this time, was that of a careless young man—not very well educated, and very saucy and insolent to his father. Smith, and his father, with several other "money-diggers" boarded at my house while they were employed in digging for a mine that they supposed had been opened and worked by the Spaniards, many years since. Young Smith gave the "money-diggers" great encouragement, at first, but when they had arrived in digging, to near the place where he had stated an immense treasure would be found—he said the enchantment was so powerful that he couldn't see.[15]

Peter Ingersoll, a neighbor of the Smith family, likewise signed a statement that gives insight into Smith's character.

In the month of August, 1827, I was hired by Joseph Smith, Jr. to go to Pennsylvania, to move his wife's household furniture to Manchester, where his wife then was. When we arrived at Mr. Hale's in Harmony, Pa. from which place he had taken his wife, a scene presented itself, truly affecting. His father-in-law (Mr. Hale) addressed Joseph, in a flood of tears: "You have stolen my daughter and married her. I had much rather have followed her to her grave. You spend your time digging for money—pretend to see in a stone, and thus try to deceive people." Joseph wept, and acknowledged he could not see in a stone now, nor never could; and that his former pretensions in that respect were all false. He then promised to give up his old habits of digging for money and looking into stones. Mr. Hale told Joseph, if he would move to Pennsylvania and work for a living, he would assist him in getting into business. Joseph acceded to this proposition. I then returned with Joseph and his wife to Manchester....On our journey to Pennsylvania, we could not make the exact change at the toll gate near Ithaca. Joseph told the gate tender, that he would "hand" him the toll on return, as he was coming back in a few days. On our return, Joseph tendered to him 25 cents, the toll being 12 1/2. He did not recognize Smith, so he accordingly gave him back the 12 1/2 cents. After we passed the gate, I asked him if he did not agree to pay double gatage on our return? No, said he, I agreed to "hand" it to him, and I did, but he handed it back again.

Ingersoll, in the same affidavit, provides valuable insight into the origin of the *Book of Mormon.*

He made me his confidant and told me what daily transpired in the family of Smiths. One day he came, and greeted me with a joyful countenance. Upon asking the cause of his unusual happiness, he replied in the following language: "As I was passing, yesterday, across the woods, after a heavy shower of rain, I found, in a hollow, some beautiful white sand, that had been washed up by the water. I took off my frock, and tied up several quarts of it, and then went home. On my entering the house, I found the family at the table eating dinner. They were all anxious to know the contents of my frock. At that moment, I happened to think of what I had heard about a history found in Canada, called the golden Bible; so I very gravely told them it was the golden Bible. To my surprise, they were credulous enough to believe what I said. Accordingly I told them I had received a commandment to let no one see it, for, says I, no man can see it with the naked eye and live. However, I offered to take out the book and show it to them, but they refused to see it and left the room.

Ingersoll went on to say that Smith made a wooden chest and put it in a pillow case, telling people that it contained the golden Bible.[16]

Many other sworn statements were collected during this era painting the same picture of Smith's character. In fact, there is not an affidavit by even one non-Mormon contemporary of Smith which sympathetically evaluates the man.

The apostles and prophets, during the earliest days of Christianity, were not accused of being rank charlatans. The most severe criticism during the dawning of the Christian faith was that they were poor, uneducated fishermen and, as such, unworthy to speak out boldly about Jesus Christ. For example, as Peter and John stood preaching before the Jewish Sanhedrin, the ruling elite of Judea, consider the response of that educated council: "Now when they saw the boldness of Peter and John, and perceived they were unlearned and ignorant men, they marvelled; and they took knowledge of them that they had been with Jesus" (Acts 4:13).

The scene is in sharp contrast with Mormonism, in which the integrity of the founder was doubted by numerous individuals *before* the religion's inception. Early Christians realized if they were going to be influences for truth and right, they had to live moral, honest lives. They took seriously the words of Christ in Matthew 5:16, "Let your light so shine before men, that they may see your good works, and glorify your Father which is in heaven."

Fruits of Early Mormonism

Let us introduce this section with the words of Jesus in Matthew 7:15-20:

Beware of false prophets, which come to you in sheep's clothing, but inwardly they are ravening wolves. Ye shall know them by their fruits. Do men gather grapes of thorns, or figs of thistles? Even so every good tree bringeth forth good fruit; but a corrupt tree bringeth forth evil fruit. A good tree cannot bring forth evil fruit, neither can a corrupt tree bring forth good fruit. Every tree that bringeth not forth good fruit is hewn down, and cast into the fire. Wherefore by their fruits ye shall know them.

In order to determine what kind of "tree" Mormonism is, some of its fruits must be considered.

The Mormon church was officially organized on April 6, 1830, at Fayette, New York, not two weeks after the *Book of Mormon* went on sale in Palmyra, New York, bookstores. Soon thereafter, some Mormons established their church in Kirtland, Ohio. They claim the reason for this move west was to get nearer to the American Indians, whom they wished to evangelize. The actual reason seems to be that Mormons were having a very difficult time making converts to their new faith in New York, where Smith's character was known. The growth of the religion depended, then, on moving to a different part of the country.

Joseph and Emma soon followed their adherents. There the Mormons grew numerically to 16,000, and in Kirtland Joseph Smith received many supposed revelations further defining the nature and organization of the Latter-day Saint church. It was in Ohio that *Doctrine and Covenants* (then called the *Book of Commandments*), another sacred book of Mormonism, was first published. In Kirtland work was done on a revision of the King James Version of the Bible. While there, Smith received the following "revelation":

> Hearken, O ye elders of my church, saith the Lord your God, who have assembled yourselves together, according to my commandments, in this land, which is the land of Missouri, which is the land which I have appointed and consecrated for the gathering of the saints. Wherefore, this is the land of promise, and the place for the city of Zion.[17]

Responding to that "divine directive" Smith took fifty Mormons with him, and, along with other adherents from New York, established the Mormon church in Jackson County, Missouri. He returned to Kirtland, but the LDS settlers in Missouri seemed unable to avoid constant friction with the established residents. The "Saints" freely told the citizens already settled in that region that God had given them the land. They taught that God would somehow take it away from the current inhabitants and present it to the Mormons.

That such talk was extremely antagonizing to their neighbors is not surprising. As a result of such caustic assertions there was constant animosity between the Latter-day Saints and all who lived near them. In the face of the resistance they stirred up, the Mormons grew even more hostile. Lyman Wight, a prominent church leader of the era, said in a sermon that non-Mormons were "hypocrites, long-faced dupes, devils, infernal hobgoblins and ghosts...they ought to be damned and sent to hell where they belong."[18]

It was here in 1833 that Sidney Rigdon, an architect of Mormon theology, preached his famous "Salt Sermon." In it, he challenged the "Gentiles," as non-Mormons were called, to do battle with the Mormon church. He said, "It shall be us and them in a war of extermination for we will follow them until the last drop of their blood is spilled, or else they will have to exterminate us; for we will carry the seat of war to their own houses, and their own families, and one party or the other shall be utterly destroyed."[19] The "Gentiles" took Sidney up on his challenge and drove the Mormon church out of the state.

Meanwhile, the Latter-day Saints enjoyed rapid numerical growth in Kirtland. Here Smith led the church into a financial fiasco which would eventually force him out of the area. He established a bank in Kirtland "by the revelation of God," or so he claimed, naming it the "Safety Society." "The Prophet," as Smith is also known to Mormons, commanded that funds be brought to his bank and quoted Scripture to intimidate his followers into coming forward with their savings. A passage Smith used was Isaiah 60:9, with one easily identifiable addition, "Surely the isles shall wait for me, and the ships of Tarshish first, to bring thy sons from afar, their silver and their gold (not their bank notes) with them unto the name of the Lord thy God."[20] The addition, of course, is the parenthetical insertion about bank notes.

Just as the Safety Society was getting off the ground, the Ohio State Legislature wisely refused to incorporate it. That didn't deter Smith, however. He simply changed the name to the "Safety Society Anti-Banking Company." Now it was an "anti-bank," Smith reasoned, and as such needed no state approval. As a result of this debacle, tens of thousands of dollars were lost. A flurry of lawsuits was filed against the Mormon church. At one point, $150,000 was owed by Mormons to non-Mormons, and that was when the dollar was worth a great deal more than it is today.[21]

Later, Smith, motivated by a warrant for his arrest on charges of bank fraud, traveled to a Mormon settlement in Far West, Missouri. Soon after his arrival, the trouble the Saints had stirred up in Jackson County spilled over into Far West, forcing the Mormons to move to Illinois.

Next, the Mormons built the city of Nauvoo, Illinois. The municipality was well-planned and erected on the banks of the Mississippi River. Joseph Smith was at the pinnacle of his power in Nauvoo. The Illinois legislature, hungry for Mormon votes, had given him the title of Lieutenant General, and he had a private army of four thousand to back it up. Smith was the mayor of Nauvoo, and the city council was made up of leading Mormons.

At that time, Joseph Smith's polygamy doctrine was gaining momentum. He made the mistake, however, of trying to persuade the wife of Dr. R.D. Foster, a resident of Nauvoo and a Mormon, to join his growing "spiritual" harem. Foster, along with William Law, Wilson Law, and Sylvester Emmons, exposed the debauchery through their newly founded paper, the *Nauvoo Expositor*. Joseph Smith and the city council declared the paper a public nuisance, and ordered it destroyed. A portion of Smith's private army carried out the orders, burning every issue.[22]

If any one act of Joseph Smith, Jr. proved to be his undoing, this was it. In a nation which had fought hard and long for freedom of the press, and against the arbitrary search and seizure policies of the British, this deed was an affront to all for which America stood. The country was outraged by the act.

The Mormons claim to have been persecuted during this era but as we see their behavior, not theological differences, brought upon them "the wrath of the Gentiles." Charles Kelly and Hoffman Birney, in their biography of leading Danite Porter Rockwell,[23] refute decisively the Mormon claim of persecution.

> Their attitude is that they have ever, with pious resignation, turned the other cheek to those who deceitfully used them. As a matter of sober fact, however, the Latter Day Saints have never attempted to live in harmony with their neighbors. They have ever been swaggering, quarrelsome and challenging; tactless to the point of downright stupidity. Religion itself, doctrinal differences between Mormonism and the more orthodox faiths, has had little or nothing to do with the persecution which the saints assert has ever been their lot. The expulsion from Missouri, the death of the Prophet and the downfall of Nauvoo, the enforced migration to the Great Basin, were occasioned only by Mormon belligerency, defiance of law and custom, and the fundamental conviction entertained by every Latter-day Saint that to rob or cheat a Gentile was to perform a holy deed.

> Persecution has ever been the Mormon battle cry, but Joseph the Prophet and Hyrum the Patriarch might have lived to die peacefully in bed had they not so heartily encouraged the robbing of Gentile hen roosts, the stealing of cattle and horses, the pillaging of lonely homesteads. Their old age might have been truly patriarchal if Nauvoo had not been made the headquarters for the manufacture of counterfeit money and a haven for every bandit of the Mississippi River bottoms. That end would have been attained

through the exercise of a quality which the Mormons, as a people, have never possessed—a tiny modicum of common sense.[24]

Without a doubt, polygamy was the most outrageous evil of this era of Mormon history. At one point, Smith probably had over fifty "wives."[25] Some of those so-called wives were in reality wives of Mormon apostles he had conveniently sent away on mission work. In fact, several other "apostates" besides the editors of the *Nauvoo Expositor* were men whose wives Smith tried to seduce. The Reorganized church in which this author was raised denies that Smith ever advocated polygamy but the evidence is overwhelming that he did.

On June 27, 1844, an angry mob stormed the Carthage, Illinois, jail in which Joseph Smith was held, and murdered both him and his brother Hyrum. From that day forward he has worn the mantle of martyr among the Latter-day Saints. As the mob began shooting, however, Smith, with a smuggled pistol, shot back. According to *History of the Church*, "When Hyrum fell, Joseph exclaimed, 'Oh dear, brother Hyrum!' and opening the door a few inches he discharged his six shooter in the stairway (as stated before), two or three barrels of which missed fire."[26] Martyrs don't shoot back.

A while later, Brigham Young moved the main body of Smith's followers from Nauvoo to Utah. Eight of the twelve Mormon apostles, including Young, were under indictment for counterfeiting when they began their hurried migration. Interestingly enough, the crime problem in that part of Illinois diminished notably when the Mormons left.

After the Latter-day Saints were in Utah, Mormon leader John D. Lee and other adherents were ordered to murder 120 non-Mormon immigrants in what became known as the Mountain Meadows Massacre. Men, women, and children were viciously slaughtered; some were shot, others had their skulls crushed, and still others had their throats slashed. Twenty years later, Lee was convicted and executed for the crime by the United States government. In *The Confessions of John D. Lee*, he admitted to the atrocity and insisted that Brigham Young ordered it.[27]

Up to the time of his execution Lee insisted that while there were many LDS participants, he was the one Mormon that Brigham Young, to appease public outrage over the slaughter, allowed to be prosecuted. In fact, Young was suspected of, and even indicted for, other murders of "Gentiles" who got in the Mormons' way. As Salt Lake City grew during the decades following Young's death, human remains, sometimes showing evidence of violent deaths, were frequently unearthed during construction projects.

The average Mormon is not aware of these facts and should be the subject of our pity. He is very often honest, zealous and frugal. He has, however, been given, and has chosen to believe, a severely edited history of his church.

Divisions of Mormonism

It is a tremendous irony that Mormonism, which Smith claims to have established as a response to the religious division all around him, has divided into over sixty sects since its inception in 1830. There are more than twenty still in existence. The largest of the religious bodies tracing their beginning to Joseph Smith is the Church of Jesus Christ of Latter-day Saints, headquartered in Salt Lake City, Utah.

The second largest of the sects spawned by Joseph Smith is the Reorganized Church of Jesus Christ of Latter Day Saints, headquartered in Independence, Missouri. This group rejects Brigham Young as a prophet and is led by a direct descendant of Joseph Smith. The "Reorganites," as they are called by the Utah church, reject the doctrine of polygamy and many of the writings of Joseph Smith. They incorrectly believe those works were authored by Young and falsely attributed to Smith. The RLDS church does not accept the doctrine of a progressive God, the plurality of gods, and rejects the Adam-God doctrine, all of which will be discussed in the fourth chapter. They label the doctrine of blood atonement, which will also be considered later, "unchristian."[28]

RLDS adherents believe in the doctrine of baptism for the dead, but feel they are unworthy to practice it at the present.[29] This group has historically taken a more moderate stand toward blacks. The RLDS church believes it, rather than the Utah church, is the true spiritual heir of Joseph Smith. While closer to the truth than the Utah church, the Reorganized church parts ways with Christianity in its devotion to Smith as a prophet and fervent belief in certain "latter day" written revelations, including the *Book of Mormon* and *Doctrine and Covenants.*

The Church of Christ, Temple Lot, is a small splinter group which, as its name suggests, owns a lot upon which Smith prophesied a temple would one day be built. This group is also known as the Hedrickite church. It has been said that the temple lot adherents have been offered literally millions of dollars for the property by the Utah church, but refuse to sell.

The Church of Jesus Christ of Latter Day Saints, Bickertonite, has adherents primarily in Pennsylvania. The Church of Jesus Christ of Latter-day Saints, Strangite is a splinter group practicing animal sacrifice, circumcision, and worshiping on Saturday. Additionally, there are still bands of polygamous Mormons, sometimes called "Fundamentalists," continuing the practice of plural marriage. Polygamy is now being practiced in parts of Salt Lake City, Bountiful, Utah, southern Utah at the Arizona border, northern and southeastern Arizona, and Mexico.

Notes

1. Joseph Smith, Jr., *Pearl of Great Price* (Salt Lake City: The Church of Jesus Christ of Latter-day Saints, 1974), Joseph Smith 2, vs. 5, 8, 14.

2. Ibid., vs. 5, 11, 21.

3. Ibid., vs. 30-42, 48-53, 54-56.

4. Gordon Hinckley, *Truth Restored: Gospel Principles* (n.p.: Corporation of the President, The Church of Jesus Christ of Latter-day Saints, 1988), 16-17.

5. Ibid., 29-30.

6. Wesley P. Walters, *New Light on Mormon Origins from the Palmyra (N. Y.) Revival* (La Mesa, California: Utah Tract Society, 1967), 12.

7. *Apostasy and Restoration* (Salt Lake City: Corporation of the President of the Church of Jesus Christ of Latter-day Saints, 1982-83), 13.

8. Joseph Fielding Smith, *Doctrines of Salvation*, Vol. I (Salt Lake City: Bookcraft, 1954-1956), 188.

9. *Historical Magazine*, News Series, Vol. 8, number 5, November, 1870, pp. 315-316, quoted in Walter Martin, *Kingdom of the Cults* (Minneapolis: Bethany House Publishers, 1985), 170.

10. William Alexander Linn, *The Story of the Mormons From the Date of Origin to the Year 1901* (London: Macmillan Company, 1902), 9.

11. Jerald and Sandra Tanner, *Mormonism—Shadow or Reality?* (Salt Lake City: Modern Microfilm Co., 1972), 33.

12. According to David Whitmer, Smith "translated" the *Book of Mormon* by the use of a "peep stone." Whitmer, one of the three witnesses to the book, wrote after his apostasy, "I will now give you a description of the manner in which the Book of Mormon was translated. Joseph would put the seer stone into a hat, and put his face into the hat, drawing it closely around his face to exclude the light; and in the darkness the spiritual light would shine. A piece of something resembling parchment would appear, and on that appeared the writing....Thus the Book of Mormon was translated by the gift and power of God, and not by any power of man." David Whitmer, *An Address To All Believers in Christ* (Richmond, Missouri: By the author, 1887), 12.

13. Pomeroy Tucker, *The Origin, Rise and Progress of Mormonism* (New York: D. Appleton & Co., 1867), 16.

14. E.D. Howe, *Mormonism Unvailed: or, a Faithful Account of that Singular Imposition and Delusion, from its Rise to the Present Time* (Plainsville, Ohio: By the author, 1834), 261.

15. Ibid., 262-263.

16. Ibid., 234-236.

17. Joseph Smith, Jr., *Doctrine and Covenants* (Salt Lake City: The Church of Jesus Christ of Latter-day Saints, 1974), 57:1-2.

18. William Swartzell, *Mormonism Exposed, Being a Journal of Residence in Missouri from the 28th of May to the 20th of August, 1838* (Pekin, Ohio: By the author, 1840), 13.

19. Linn, *The Story of the Mormons,* 197.

20. Joseph Smith, Jr., *History of the Church of Jesus Christ of Latter-day Saints,* Vol. II., Introduction and Notes by B.H. Roberts (Salt Lake City: Deseret News, 1902-1912), copyrighted 1948 by Joseph Fielding Smith, 473.

21. Fawn M. Brodie, *No Man Knows My History* (New York: Alfred P. Knopf, 1971), 202.

22. Charles Kelly and Hoffman Birney, *Holy Murder: The Story of Porter Rockwell* (New York: Minton, Balch & Company, 1934), 61.

23. Danites were a group of men that served as bodyguards and even murdered at the bidding of first Joseph Smith and later Brigham Young. There is strong evidence that Danite Porter Rockwell was the attempted assassin of anti-Mormon Missouri Governor Lilburn Boggs.

24. Ibid., 37-38.

25. Brodie, *No Man Knows My History,* 334.

26. Smith, *History of the Church,* Vol. VI, p. 618.

27. John D. Lee, *Mormonism Unveiled: Or The Life and Confessions of the Late John D. Lee* (St. Louis: Bryan, Brand & Co., 1877), 213, 214, 218-254 and 258.

28. Russell F. Ralston, *Fundamental Differences Between the Reorganized Church and the Utah Church* (Independence, Missouri: Herald Publishing House, 1963), 127.

29. Ibid., 209.

Chapter 2

The Book of Mormon

Upon examining the *Book of Mormon*, we are struck with a sense of surprise that the crude and unusual publication ever gained a following. Alexander Campbell, a leading religious figure of the early nineteenth century, wrote the first thorough review of the book. Campbell ended his critique with the following comment:

> Such is an analysis of the *Book of Mormon*, the Bible of the Mormonites. For noticing of which I would have asked forgiveness from all my readers, had not several hundred persons of different denominations believed in it. On this account alone had it become necessary to notice it, and for the same reason we must examine its pretensions to divine authority; for it purports to be a revelation from God.[1]

Since that statement was made, believers in the *Book of Mormon* have become one of the fastest-growing religious movements in the world. The same purpose that caused Campbell to evaluate the book serves, then, as an even greater motivation to us.

The *Book of Mormon*, a fifteen-chapter volume organized in a manner similar to the Bible, is the cornerstone of the

Church of Jesus Christ of Latter-day Saints. Mormons place tremendous credibility in it. The *Pearl of Great Price* asserts in Article 8 of the Articles of Faith, "We also believe the *Book of Mormon* to be the word of God." In fact, Latter-day Saints believe it is more accurate than the Bible. Smith declared, "The *Book of Mormon* is the most correct of any book on earth."[2] While the Mormons accept the Bible "insofar as it is correctly translated," no such qualification is placed on the *Book of Mormon*.

Early LDS apostle Orson Pratt spoke of the critical role the *Book of Mormon* would play in the lives of many. He stated in the first of a series of tracts entitled *Divine Authenticity of the Book of Mormon* in 1850:

> This book must be either true or false. If true, it is one of the most important messages ever sent from God...If false, it is one of the most cunning, wicked, bold, deep-laid impositions ever palmed upon the world, calculated to deceive and ruin millions who would sincerely receive it as the word of God, and will suppose themselves securely built upon the rock of truth until they are plunged with their families into hopeless despair.

> The nature of the message in the *Book of Mormon* is such, that if true, no one can possibly be saved and reject it; if false, no one can possibly be saved and receive it.

With those words we heartily agree. If true, the *Book of Mormon* would be the most important document of modern times. It would be deserving of our closest scrutiny and careful obedience. If true, it should be found in every church, college, house, hospital, hotel and motel room in the world. But if the volume is false, its vicious deceptiveness will spell destruction for millions of souls. Let's consider the *Book of Mormon* in light of Orson Pratt's statement.

The Story of the *Book of Mormon*

The *Book of Mormon* primarily contains the purported history of two ancient civilizations in the Americas begun by immigrants from Bible lands. The first of these civilizations was launched by a group of sojourners who began their trek at the time of the Tower of Babel, around 2250 B.C. according to Mormon chronology. They took with them fowls, fish, and swarms of bees. The pilgrims came to a great sea where they built barges in order to cross it. Upon completion of the vessels they sailed. After 344 days they all landed on the same day and at the same place at the "promised land"—the eastern coast of Central America. Known as the Jaredites, they fought among themselves until all were killed.

A second group of immigrants consisted of righteous Jews whose leader was Nephi. They came to America about 600 B.C., eventually dividing into two warring camps, the Nephites and the Lamanites. The Lamanites, cursed by God with dark skin because of their rebellious ways, became the ancestors of American Indians. The evil Lamanites grew more powerful than their righteous neighbors and finally destroyed the Nephites in a decisive battle at the Hill of Cumorah in A.D. 428, near what would later be known as Palmyra, New York. Fourteen hundred years after that final battle, Joseph Smith, Jr. was given the record of these ancient peoples by the angel Moroni, the son of Mormon, an author of the *Book of Mormon*. The title page of the original 1830 edition of the *Book of Mormon* says, however, "By Joseph Smith, Jr., Author and Proprietor."[3]

The Real Story of the *Book of Mormon*

What is the real story of the *Book of Mormon?* Probably this: a retired minister, Solomon Spaulding, wrote historical romances in a Biblical style. One such novel was entitled *Manuscript Found*. Somehow, Joseph Smith obtained the manuscript and enlarged upon it. In fact, witnesses acquainted with Spaulding, upon reading the *Book of Mormon*, said it sounded very much like *Manuscript Found*. But even if the *Book of Mormon* was not authored in large part by

Solomon Spaulding, even if it is not *Manuscript Found*, even if the true author of the *Book of Mormon* is never known, we can still know that it is not from God.

The *Book of Mormon* Has No Credible Witnesses

Proof that the *Book of Mormon* is genuine is, to Mormons, found in the statements of three, then eight, witnesses at the front of each copy. "The Testimony of the Three Witnesses" reads:

> BE IT KNOWN unto all nations, kindreds, tongues, and people, unto whom this work shall come: That we, through the grace of God the Father, and our Lord Jesus Christ, have seen the plates which contain this record, which is a record of the people of Nephi, and also of the Lamanites, their brethren, and also of the people of Jared, who came from the tower of which hath been spoken. And we also know that they have been translated by the gift and power of God, for his voice hath declared it unto us; wherefore we know of a surety that the work is true. And we also testify that we have seen the engravings which are upon the plates; and they have been shown unto us by the power of God, and not of man. And we declare with words of soberness, that an angel of God came down from heaven, and he brought and laid before our eyes, that we beheld and saw the plates, and the engravings thereon; and we know that it is by the grace of God the Father, and our Lord Jesus Christ, that we beheld and bear record that these things are true. And it is marvelous in our eyes. Nevertheless, the voice of the Lord commanded us that we should bear record of it; wherefore, to be obedient unto the commandments of God, we bear testimony of these things. And we know that if we are faithful in Christ, we shall rid our garments of the blood of all men, and be found spotless before the judgment-seat of Christ, and shall dwell with him eternally in the heavens. And the honor be to the Father, and to the Son, and to the Holy Ghost, which is one God. Amen.
>
> Oliver Cowdery
> David Whitmer
> Martin Harris[4]

This is obviously a very strong statement in support of the *Book of Mormon*. What the Mormon church fails to point out, however, is that all three witnesses later apostatized from the Mormon church. In *Journal of Discourses*, Mormon apostle George A. Smith related the following,

> After the organization of the Twelve Apostles, and the so far finishing of the Kirtland Temple as to hold a solemn assembly...the spirit of apostacy [sic] became more general,...One of the First Presidency, several of the Twelve Apostles, High Council, President of the Seventies, *the witnesses of the Book of Mormon* [italics added], Presidents of Far West, and a number of others standing high in the church were all carried away in this apostacy [sic]....[5]

Joseph Smith, Jr. likewise, wrote in a letter dated December 16, 1838, "Such characters as...John Whitmer, David Whitmer, Oliver Cowdery, and Martin Harris are too mean to mention; and we had liked to have forgotten them."[6] In fact, they are called "thieves and counterfeiters" in other Mormon records. So much for them. "The Testimony of the Eight Witnesses" will now be considered.

> BE IT KNOWN unto all nations, kindreds, tongues, and people, unto whom this work shall come: That Joseph Smith, Jun., the translator of this work, has shown unto us the plates of which hath been spoken, which have the appearance of gold; and as many of the leaves as the said Smith has translated we did handle with our hands; and we also saw the engravings thereon, all of which has the appearance of ancient work, and of curious workmanship. And this we bear record with words of soberness, that the said Smith has shown unto us, for we have seen and hefted, and know of a surety that the said Smith has got the plates of which we have spoken. And we give our names unto the world, to witness unto the world that which we have seen. And we lie not, God bearing witness of it.

Christian Whitmer	Hiram Page
Jacob Whitmer	Joseph Smith, Sen.
Peter Whitmer, Jun.	Hyrum Smith
John Whitmer	Samuel H. Smith[7]

Even some of those men were later denigrated by the Mormon church. We have already seen the opinion that was held concerning John Whitmer, and Hiram Page was considered to be fanatical.[8] It should also be noted that three of the witnesses were members of Joseph Smith's family. Four of the eight witnesses were Whitmers, related to David Whitmer, and Hiram Page had married a Whitmer. Mark Twain observed, "I could not feel more satisfied and at rest if the entire Whitmer family had testified."[9]

Even disregarding the lack of credibility of these men, we are still left with an amazing fact. The eight witnesses did not claim to have seen golden plates miraculously given to Joseph Smith, or to have witnessed any supernatural event, for that matter. They simply claimed to see some plates that had "the appearance of gold." These witnesses only surmised that the "ancient records" were miraculously delivered. Apparently "The Prophet" was pressed to provide some evidence for his claim of having found plates with the aid of a divine messenger. He responded to the pressure by producing something that looked like the plates he had talked about so much.

An examination of the testimonies still leaves us totally without credible witnesses to the supernatural events which Smith claimed were the foundation of the Mormon church.

The *Book of Mormon* Defies Archaeology

Mormons are increasingly faced with the fact that archaeology doesn't back up the *Book of Mormon*. A brochure issued by Brigham Young University advertising travel study tours to Central and South America for the 1990-1991 academic year states, "Though we cannot speak authoritatively or precisely about the location of *Book of Mormon* sites, we can—by a visit to Mesoamerica—create a mental tapestry resembling the land and circumstances in which the story actually occurred."[10] Those words demonstrate the candor that has been forced upon educated Mormons by archaeology. The location of *Book of Mormon* sites cannot be spoken of "authoritatively or precisely" because scientific evidence overwhelmingly demonstrates that they do not exist.

Some Mormon authorities have tried to deal with the lack of evidence for the *Book of Mormon* by asserting that archaeological findings are so vague that no one can be quite sure what took place in the Americas. Hugh Nibley, Mormonism's foremost apologist, wrote, "There are no natural laws by which the social scientist can tell whether events and situations described in the *Book of Mormon* were real or not. All we have is a huge heap of ancient records which will indicate more or less whether such things were plausible or possible."[11] Nibley's statement is out of touch with reality because there is more than a "heap" of ancient records. There is an enormous amount of evidence, both in ancient records and in the ruins of ancient cities, which tells more than enough about the civilizations with which the *Book of Mormon* allegedly deals. That evidence proves the volume is false.

The *Book of Mormon* portrays massive populations and grand civilizations in the Americas. In Jarom 1:8 we read:

> And we multiplied exceedingly, and spread upon the face of the land, and became exceedingly rich in gold, and in silver, and in precious things, and in fine workmanship of wood, in buildings, and in machinery, and also in iron and copper, and brass and steel, making all manner of tools of every kind to till the ground, and weapons of war—yea, the sharp pointed arrow, and the quiver, and the dart, and the javelin, and all preparations for war.

Likewise, the *Book of Mormon* declares in Mormon 1:7, "The whole face of the land had become covered with buildings, and the people were as numerous almost, as it were the sand of the sea." According to Ether 9:23, they "did build many cities." The *Book of Mormon* mentions extensive shipping, temple-building, all types of tools and gold and silver coinage. Helaman 3:14 refers to "their shipping, and their building of ships, and their building of temples, and of synagogues and their sanctuaries." Weapons manufacturing had developed into a sophisticated skill. Alma 43:18-19 mentions "swords...cimeters [sic]...weapons of war...breast-plates...arm-shields...shields."

Steel was even known in the Americas long before it was discovered in any other part of the world. According to the *Book of Mormon*, Nephi gave Laban a sword with a blade "of the most precious steel" (1 Nephi 4:9). According to this so-called inspired record, the population of the Americas was so vast that in one decisive battle alone, more people lost their lives than in any other battle in the history of the world.

> And it came to pass when Coriantumr had recovered of his wounds, he began to remember the words which Ether had spoken unto him. He saw that there had been slain by the sword already nearly two millions of his people, and he began to sorrow in his heart; yea there had been slain two millions of mighty men, and also their wives and their children [Ether 15:1-2].

According to the *Book of Mormon*, the immigrants to the Americas had horses and livestock. It is asserted in Ether 9:18-19 that these included the following:

> ...all manner of cattle, of oxen, and cows, and of sheep, and of swine, and of goats, and also many other kinds of animals which were useful for the food of man. And they also had horses, and asses, and there were elephants and cureloms and cumoms; all of which were useful unto man, and more especially the elephants and cureloms and cumoms.

Over the years, various scholars have gone on record exposing these untruths. Wm. Duncan Strong, of the Department of Anthropology at Columbia University, wrote in a letter in 1957, responding to questions about the *Book of Mormon*, "I do not believe that there is a single thing of value concerning the prehistory of the American Indian in the *Book of Mormon* and I believe the great majority of American archaeologists would agree with me. The book is untrue biblically, historically and scientifically."[12]

Except for the cureloms and cumoms which apparently existed only in the imagination of Joseph Smith, it is universally accepted that Spaniards brought domesticated animals to the New World. A statement from no less than the Smithsonian Institution, dated January 1987, says:

> 1. The Smithsonian Institution has never used the *Book of Mormon* in any way as a scientific guide. Smithsonian archaeologists see no direct connection between the archaeology of the New World and the subject matter of the book.

> 2. The physical type of the American Indian is basically Mongoloid, being most closely related to that of the peoples of eastern, central, and northeastern Asia. Archaeological evidence indicates that the ancestors of the present Indians came into the New World—probably over a land bridge known to have existed in the Bering Strait region during the last Ice Age....

> 3. Present evidence indicates that the first people to reach this continent from the East were the Norsemen who briefly visited the northeastern part of North America around A.D. 1000 and then settled in Greenland. There is nothing to show that they reached Mexico or Central America.

> 4. One of the main lines of evidence supporting the scientific finding that contacts with Old World civilizations, if indeed they occurred at all, were of very little significance for the development of American Indian civilizations, is the fact that none of the principal Old World domesticated food plants or animals (except the dog) occurred in the New World in pre-Columbian times. American Indians had no wheat, barley, oats, millet, rice, cattle, pigs, chickens, horses, donkeys, camels before 1492.

> 5. Iron, steel, glass, and silk were not used in the New World before 1492 (except for occasional use of unsmelted meteoric iron). Native copper was worked in various locations in pre-Columbian times, but true metallurgy was limited to southern Mexico and the Andean region, where its occurrence in late

prehistoric times involved gold, silver, copper, and their alloys, but not iron.

6. There is a possibility that the spread of cultural traits across the Pacific to Mesoamerica and the northwestern coast of South America began several hundred years before the Christian era. However, any such inter-hemispheric contacts appear to have been the results of accidental voyages originating in eastern and southern Asia. It is by no means certain that even such contacts occurred; certainly there were no contacts with the ancient Egyptians, Hebrews, or other peoples of Western Asia and the Near East.

7. No reputable Egyptologist or other specialist on Old World archaeology, and no expert on New World prehistory, has discovered or confirmed any relationship between archaeological remains in Mexico and archaeological remains in Egypt.

8. Reports of findings of ancient Egyptian, Hebrew, and other Old World writings in the New World in pre-Columbian contexts have frequently appeared in newspapers, magazines, and sensational books. None of these claims has stood up to examination by reputable scholars. No inscriptions using Old World forms of writing have been shown to have occurred in any part of the Americas before 1492 except for a few Norse rune stones which have been found in Greenland.[13]

Even the great Smithsonian Institution has gone on record as declaring the lack of historicity of the *Book of Mormon*, declared by Joseph Smith, Jr. as being "the most correct of any book on earth, and the keystone of our religion [by which] a man would get closer to God by abiding its precepts, than by any other book."[14] One author correctly observed that the array of inaccuracies in the book "stamps it as written by someone who knew nothing about ancient America and presumed that no one ever would know."

In stark contrast, virtually all the archaeology of the Bible has been verified repeatedly. In fact, it has even been used by archaeologists as a guide in locating ancient ruins. Merrill Unger wrote, "Old Testament archaeology has rediscovered whole nations, resurrected important peoples, and in a most astonishing manner filled in historical gaps, adding immeasurably to the knowledge of biblical backgrounds."[15]

The Mormon claim that the *Book of Mormon* was written in reformed Egyptian is particularly out of harmony with archaeological facts concerning the language used by the Jews. In Mormon 9:32-33, the *Book of Mormon* states:

> And now, behold, we have written this record according to our knowledge, in the characters which are called among us the reformed Egyptian, being handed down and altered by us, according to our manner of speech. And if our plates had been sufficiently large we should have written in Hebrew...and if we could have written in Hebrew, behold we have had no imperfection in our record.

M.T. Lamb, author of *The Golden Bible*, stated concerning the absurdities of the supposed use of "reformed Egyptian":

> There are a multitude of reasons that make such [usage] altogether improbable. In the first place, Lehi had lived all his lifetime, "in all his days"...in the city of Jerusalem, surrounded constantly by those who spoke only the Hebrew language. Had he been an Egyptian by birth, and with loving tenderness clung to his native tongue, the above statement would have a very different look. But Lehi was a Hebrew, a pure Hebrew, was born and reared in the city of Jerusalem, with family relationships and social surroundings all Hebraistic. In the second place, the Jews hated the Egyptians with a bitter hatred, and it is therefore inconceivable that a true-born Jew, a real lover of his own people, loyal and patriotic as he professes to have been, would have been willing thus to insult his people, or that the Jews around him would have endured the insult. In the third place, the ancient Jew had an unusual veneration for his mother tongue, the sacred Hebrew, the most ancient language upon earth, as he believed; the loved tongue of his illustrious ancestry....But in the fourth place, God's will had been very clearly expressed upon a multitude of occasions as to the propriety of having any intercourse with the Egyptians or longings for anything to be found there.[16]

Nephi, son of Lehi and the one who did the record-keeping for the family, wrote in 600 B.C., according to the date given in the *Book of Mormon* that he recorded in "the language of the Egyptians" (1 Nephi 1:2). At this time, as Lamb pointed out, the Egyptians and Jews were adversaries. In fact, King Josiah of Judea was killed in a battle with Egypt about the time of Nephi, and the Jews then began paying tribute to Egypt (2 Chronicles 35:20-36:4). Combine those truths with the indisputable fact that "Reformed Egyptian" has never existed as a language and the absurdity of the entire Mormon claim is evident. One author observed:

> What assurance have we, then, that "Reformed Egyptian" was actually spoken and actually written? We must simply take one man's word for this: namely, that of Joseph Smith. Further, the existence of manuscripts in the original languages of the Bible and the existence of an extra-Biblical literature in these languages enable Biblical scholars to study the grammar of these languages and to engage in lexicographical studies. All of this type of study, however, is impossible in the case of "Reformed Egyptian." Why do we have no lexicons of "Reformed Egyptian," no grammars of "Reformed Egyptian," as we do have Hebrew lexicons and Hebrew grammars, Greek lexicons and Greek grammars? Does it seem likely that God went to all the trouble of having these additional revelations recorded in "Reformed Egyptian," only to allow all further traces of this language to disappear?[17]

Clearly, the claim that Smith was given "golden plates" which were inscribed in "Reformed Egyptian" is patently false.

The *Book of Mormon* Defies Common Sense

We can know the *Book of Mormon* is not from God because it violates common sense. It is absurdly stated in Ether 2:16-17 concerning the eight vessels in which the immigrants were to travel to the New World:

And the Lord said: Go to work and build, after the manner of barges which ye have hitherto built. And it came to pass that the brother of Jared did go to work, and also his brethren, and built barges after the manner which they had built, according to the instructions of the Lord. And they were small and they were light upon the water, even like unto the likeness of a fowl upon the water. And they were built after a manner that they were exceeding tight, even that they would hold water like unto a dish; and the bottom thereof was tight like unto a dish; and the sides thereof were tight like unto a dish; and the ends thereof were peaked; and the top thereof was tight like unto a dish; and length thereof was the length of a tree; and the door thereof, when it was shut, was tight like unto a dish.

Consider the phrase, "And the length thereof was the length of a tree." In all of literature, surely, there is not a more meaningless description. The length of these vessels is here said to be somewhere between that of a two-inch seedling and a three-hundred foot Giant Sequoia. In other words, absolutely nothing is said.

The barges were built "according to the instructions of the Lord." Apparently the Lord can't build too well, as they had two outstanding deficiencies. The first was noticed by the brother of Jared, or so the *Book of Mormon* has it. He was concerned about the airtight nature of the ships, asking upon completion, "And also we shall perish, for in them we cannot breathe, save it is the air which is in them" (Ether 2:19). In verse 20, God responds, "Behold, thou shalt make a hole in the top, and also in the bottom; and when thou shalt suffer for air thou shalt unstop the hole and receive air. And if it be so that the water come in upon thee, behold, ye shall stop the hole, that ye may not perish in the flood."

To paraphrase, Jared complains, "These vessels are tight like unto a dish—we won't be able to breathe." The Lord supposedly answers, "Make a hole in the top and the bottom and stop them up. When you start suffocating because of a lack of air, unstop one of the holes. If water comes gushing in, you have the wrong hole. You need to plug that one back up and unplug the other one!"

The Lord, it seems, also forgot about lighting, because Jared again complained, according to Ether 2:22, "Behold, O Lord, wilt thou suffer that we shall cross this great water in darkness?" The Lord then asked Jared what he would want done to solve the problem (2:25). Jared, seemingly able to imaginatively handle any emergency, "went forth unto the mount, which they called the mount Shelem, because of its exceeding height, and did molten out of a rock sixteen small stones; and they were white and clear, even as transparent glass" (3:1). Jared then asked, "Touch these stones, O Lord, with thy finger, and prepare them that they may shine forth in darkness" (3:4). The Lord complied and the lighting crisis was resolved. Two stones were placed in every barge, one at each end of the vessels. In this author's opinion, the words "patently ridiculous" seem too kind.

Consider further that as the immigrants sailed for the New World, they took with them livestock, birds, fish and even bees! In the book of Ether chapter 2 verses 1-3 we read:

> And it came to pass that Jared and his brother, and their families, and also the friends of Jared and his brother and their families, went down into the valley which was northward, (and the name of the valley was Nimrod, being called after the mighty hunter) with their flocks which they had gathered together, male and female, of every kind. And they did also lay snares and catch fowls of the air; and they did also prepare a vessel, in which they did carry with them the fish of the waters. And they did also carry with them deseret, which, by interpretation, is a honey bee; and thus they did carry with them swarms of bees, and all manner of that which was upon the face of the land, seeds of every kind.

Thus we have airtight vessels the length of a tree, lit by glowing rocks, in which beehives, fish and livestock, as well as humans, traveled to the Americas. Nephi even had a compass for his voyage, yet none existed at that time (they weren't in use in the Western World until the twelfth century A.D.).

In 1 Nephi chapter 22:21 the *Book of Mormon* says that Christ "was the Holy One of Israel," yet Jesus would not be born for hundreds of years after those words were supposedly spoken, according to Mormon chronology. Alma 30:2 says, "In the sixteenth year of the reign of the judges over the people of Nephi there began to be continual peace." On the other hand, Alma 35:13 says that in the eighteenth year of the reign of the judges, "Thus commenced a war betwixt the Lamanites and the Nephites." That is quite a period of continual peace—two years!

Another example of the defiance of common sense typical of the *Book of Mormon* is seen in the time it assigns for the establishment of Christ's church and the use of the term "Christian." In Matthew 16:18, Jesus says, "I will build my church," speaking of it in future tense. Yet Mosiah 18:17, dated 147 B.C., says, "And they were called the church of God, or the church of Christ, from that time forward." Imagine, Christ had a church one hundred and fifty years before his birth! The Bible teaches that followers of Christ were "called Christians first in Antioch" (Acts 11:26). Yet, according to Alma 46:15, there were Christians in 73 B.C. In other words, there were Christians before Christ. Now that is quite an accomplishment!

The very area in which the *Book of Mormon* adventure supposedly took place raises serious questions when evaluated in the light of mere common sense. Almost all the historic part of the book is alleged to have occurred in Central America or Mexico. Yet, strangely enough, the saga closes in western New York state, where the massive, final battle between Lamanites and Nephites is supposed to have taken place. Why an immense number of disputants traveled all the way to New England for their final showdown is one of the unexplained mysteries of the *Book of Mormon*.

One of the most absurd teachings of the *Book of Mormon* is the doctrine that God's curse of dark skin upon the Lamanites is why American Indians have dark complexions. Of Nephites who became Lamanites the *Book of Mormon* asserts, "The Lord God did cause a skin of blackness to come upon them" (2 Nephi 5:21). When they were converted, their skin lightened. "Their curse was taken from them, and their skin became white like unto the Nephites" (3 Nephi 2:15). In response to this teaching, Latter-day Saints early in their history did a great deal of mission work among American Indians, and converted many. Even though today there are third, forth and even fifth-generation Indian Mormons, there is not an instance of even one ever experiencing a lightening of the skin upon submitting to the "gospel according to Joseph Smith."

That the *Book of Mormon* is at variance with common sense is again demonstrated in an account of hand-to-hand combat found in Ether 15:30-31, which says:

> And it came to pass that when Coriantumr had leaned upon his sword, that he rested for a little, he smote off the head of Shiz. And it came to pass that after he had smitten off the head of Shiz, that Shiz raised upon his hands and fell; and after that he had struggled for breath, he died.

Considering that he had been decapitated, Shiz was very energetic!

Another glaring example of the conflict between common sense and the *Book of Mormon* is seen in the French word *adieu* found in Jacob 7:27. It is claimed that the book was miraculously translated from reformed Egyptian into English, yet here God apparently chose to render a word in French. According to dates given in the *Book of Mormon*, Jacob was written between 544 and 421 B.C. The French language didn't exist until A.D. 700, making the use of that word doubly ridiculous. These New World Jews, according to 3 Nephi 9:18, also included the Greek terms *alpha* and *omega* in their reformed Egyptians records.

The method of ascertaining the truth of the *Book of Mormon* defies common sense. Moroni 10:4 states:

> And when ye shall receive these things, I would exhort you that ye would ask God, the Eternal Father, in the name of Christ, if these things are not true; and if ye shall ask with a sincere heart, with real intent, having faith in Christ, he will manifest the truth of it unto you, by the power of the Holy Ghost.

Mormons place a lot of confidence in the "burning bosom" which they experience as a result of obeying this command. What we have here, however, is a blatant case of circular reasoning. One has to first believe the *Book of Mormon* in order to accept that command and pray accordingly. In other words, for the *Book of Mormon* to be proved, it must first be accepted as true.

While prayer is an important tool for Christians, some things are so obvious they can be determined without prayer. One author observed:

> Christians ought to pray much but there are some things about which they do not need to pray. The reason is that the evidence is already so clear that prayer would accomplish nothing. Are you married? If you are you know it and if you aren't you know it, so it is foolish to pray and ask God to show you whether or not you are married. Have you ever read a Mother Goose rhyme? Is it necessary to pray and ask God whether or not it is scripture? Now that is so absurd that it may sound sacrilegious, but it does illustrate the fact that it is not necessary to pray about every book which someone claims is scripture.[18]

As we have seen thus far, there is much evidence that the *Book of Mormon* did not come from God. Clearly, prayer is not necessary to determine its origin.

The *Book of Mormon* Defies Grammar

We know the *Book of Mormon* is not from God because it defies English grammar. Over 4,000 changes have been made since the original 1830 edition. Some are doctrinal. For example, 1 Nephi 11:18 originally stated, "Behold, the virgin which thou seest is the mother of God." The passage now reads "mother of the Son of God." 1 Nephi 11:21 originally said, "Behold the Lamb of God, yea, even the Eternal Father!" The same verse in more recent editions reads "even the Son of the Eternal Father." In the first edition of the *Book of Mormon*, 1 Nephi 11:32 said, "And I looked and beheld the Lamb of God, that he was taken by the people; yea, the everlasting God was judged of the world." The passage now reads "yea, the Son of the everlasting God was judged of the world."

Many changes were made to correct the poor grammar permeating the original *Book of Mormon*. Following are a few examples of statements found in the 1830 edition which are changed in current editions. "My father had read and saw" has been altered to "my father had read and seen." "The tender mercies of the Lord is" has been changed to "the tender mercies of the Lord are." "Thy power, and goodness, and mercy is over all the inhabitants of the earth" has been changed to "thy power, and goodness and mercy are over all the inhabitants of the earth."

In spite of massive modifications, grammatical errors still remain in the 1981 edition of the *Book of Mormon*. In Helaman 1:7 we read, "Therefore, he was about to flatter away those people to rise up in rebellion against their brethren." Smith apparently thought the phrase, "flatter away" meant "instigate." In Alma 27:4, the *Book of Mormon* says, "Now when Ammon and his brethren saw this work of destruction among those whom they so dearly beloved, and among those who so dearly beloved them." We do not "dearly belove" people we "dearly love" them.

In Helaman 9:6 the *Book of Mormon* says, "Now, immediately when the judge had been murdered—he being stabbed by his brother by a garb of secrecy." "Garb" is clothing; one can't be stabbed with a piece of clothing. A "garb of secrecy" is a figurative piece of clothing—it would be even move difficult for someone to be stabbed with that!

Errors in grammar in the *Book of Mormon* might be excusable if it only claimed to be a human translation. In fact, the reason given for these errors is that Smith was uneducated. That excuse is unacceptable because the *Book of Mormon* is claimed to have been translated with God literally choosing every word and Joseph Smith dictating the words as they miraculously appeared to him. All of the grammatical errors in the book, by Mormon reasoning, must be laid at the feet of God.

Alexander Campbell, commenting on the writing style of the volume, wisely stated, "I would as soon compare a bat to the American eagle...as to contrast it with a single chapter in all the writings of the Jewish or Christian prophets."[19]

The *Book of Mormon* Defies Mormonism

We know the *Book of Mormon* is not from God because it is even in conflict with Mormonism. It contradicts the Mormon doctrine of polygamy. In Jacob 2:26-28 we read:

> Wherefore, I the Lord God will not suffer that this people shall do like unto them of old. Wherefore, my brethren, hear me, and hearken to the word of the Lord: For there shall not any man among you have save it be one wife; and concubines he shall have none; For I, the Lord God, delight in the chastity of women. And whoredoms are an abomination before me; thus saith the Lord of Hosts.

Notice that polygamy is forbidden because it is directly in conflict with the "chastity of women." Polygamous unions are further identified as "whoredoms" and "an abomination" to God. It is difficult to imagine a stronger, clearer condemnation of plural marriage. In Ether 10:5, the *Book of Mormon* says, "And it came to pass that Riplakish did not do that which was right in the sight of the Lord, for he did have many wives and concubines." There a man is specifically said to be displeasing to God because of a plurality of wives.

The *Book of Mormon* contradicts the Mormon doctrine of a plurality of gods which will be examined in greater detail later. Ether 2:8 describes Deity as singular, stating, "And he had sworn in his wrath unto the brother of Jared, that whoso should possess this land of promise, from that time henceforth and forever, should serve him, the true and only God, or they should be swept off when the fullness of his wrath should come upon them."

The *Book of Mormon* contradicts the Mormon teaching that baptism is not essential for salvation. *Doctrine and Covenants* 20:37 asserts that remission of sins precedes baptism, declaring, "All who humble themselves...and truly manifest by their works that they have received of the Spirit of Christ unto the remission of their sins, shall be received by baptism into his church." Yet the *Book of Mormon* teaches remission of sins is conditional on baptism. It states, "Yea, blessed are they who shall believe in your words, and come down into the depths of humility and be baptized, for they...shall...receive a remission of their sins" (3 Nephi 12:2).

The *Book of Mormon* teaches that death seals man's fate. Alma 34:33 says, "If we do not improve our time while in this life, then cometh the night of darkness wherein there can be no labor performed." Yet *Doctrine and Covenants* 88:99 teaches that the lost will have a second chance, declaring, "Another angel shall sound, which is the second trump; and then cometh the redemption of those who are Christ's at his coming; who have received their part in that prison which is prepared for them, that they might receive the gospel, and be judged according to men in the flesh."

Joseph Smith claimed that the *Book of Mormon* is "the most correct of any book."[20] Likewise, according to *Doctrine and Covenants* 27:5, the *Book of Mormon* contains the fullness of the everlasting gospel. Yet it does not contain the Mormon doctrine of the priesthood of Melchizedek, a bedrock doctrine of the Mormon church. It does not contain the Mormon doctrine that God is an exalted man. It does not contain the Mormon doctrine of celestial marriage. It does not contain the Mormon doctrine of baptism for the dead or the "Word of Wisdom"—that body of LDS teaching that forbids the use of tobacco, liquor, etc. The *Book of Mormon* does not contain many other doctrines of Mormonism.

The *Book of Mormon* Defies the Bible

Finally, we know the *Book of Mormon* is not from God because it defies the Bible. Actually, it doesn't always contradict the Bible; sometimes it agrees with it too much. Careful study has revealed that over 25,000 words in the *Book of Mormon* have been plagiarized from the King James Version. In fact, several long passages have been lifted out of the Bible and plugged almost verbatim into the *Book of Mormon*. Consider, for example, what the Bible says in Isaiah 4:1-3:

> And in that day seven women shall take hold of one man, saying, We will eat our own bread, and wear our own apparel: only let us be called by thy name, to take away our reproach. In that day shall the branch of the Lord be beautiful and glorious, and the fruit of the earth shall be excellent and comely for them that are escaped of Israel. And it shall come to pass, that he that is left in Zion, and he that remaineth in Jerusalem, shall be called holy, even everyone that is written among the living in Jerusalem.

Compare that to 2 Nephi chapter 14:1-3 of the *Book of Mormon*:

And in that day, seven women shall take hold of one man, saying:
We will eat our own bread, and wear our own apparel; only let us
be called by thy name to take away our reproach. In that day shall
the branch of the Lord be beautiful and glorious; the fruit of the
earth excellent and comely to them that are escaped of Israel. And
it shall come to pass, they that are left in Zion and remain in
Jerusalem shall be called holy, every one that is written among
the living in Jerusalem.

The Isaiah passage is reproduced in the *Book of Mormon*
with nearly word-for-word exactness! Another example of
flagrant plagiarism is found in Moroni 10:8-17 which is
suspiciously close to 1 Corinthians 12:4-11. Similarly,
Mosiah chapter 14 is a reproduction of Isaiah 53 and 3 Nephi
13:1-23 copies Matthew 6:1-23. Many other examples of
plagiarism of the King James Version of the Bible are found
in the *Book of Mormon*, "the most correct of any book."

Where the Bible has not been plagiarized, many clumsy
errors can be found. For example, according to Alma 7:10,
Christ "shall be born of Mary, at Jerusalem." Every school-
boy and schoolgirl knows Christ was born in Bethlehem
(Micah 5:2). A similar error is found in Helaman 12:25-26
where John 5:29 is loosely quoted. The *Book of Mormon*
says, "But we read that in the great and last day there are
some who shall be cast out...: they that have done good shall
have everlasting life: and they that have done evil shall have
everlasting damnation." The problem here is that according
to Latter-day Saint chronology, Helaman was written in 6
B.C., several decades before the writing of any New Testament book.

Helaman 14:20, 27 says that the earth would be darkened
for three days at Jesus' death. The Bible, on the other hand,
teaches the darkness lasted three hours. Matthew 27:45 declares, "Now from the sixth hour there was darkness over all
the land unto the ninth hour." Alma 13:18 states, "Melchizedek...did reign under his father." Yet the Bible plainly

teaches Melchizedek was a one-time priest who therefore reigned under no one. According to Hebrews 7:3, Melchizedek was "without father, without mother, without descent, having neither beginning of days, nor end of life; but made like unto the Son of God; [and] abideth a priest continually."

The very existence of the *Book of Mormon* contradicts the Bible. Long before the nineteenth century when golden plates were supposedly given to Joseph Smith, the apostle Peter wrote that God's "divine power hath given unto us all things that pertain unto life and godliness" (2 Peter 1:3). Humankind was fully-equipped with all necessary spiritual information eighteen hundred years before Smith was born.

Conclusion

Even if the *Book of Mormon* didn't defy archaeology, or common sense, or rules of grammar, or Mormonism, or the Bible itself, we would still know that it is not from God. In Jude 3 the Bible says, "Earnestly contend for the faith which was once delivered unto the saints." The word translated "once" in the original Greek is *hapax*, which literally means "once for all." There have not been two deliveries of the faith, one in Bible lands and the other in the Americas, but only one delivery, and that in the first century. And the record of that faith provided once for all time rests before us in the pages of the New Testament.

Notes

1. Alexander Campbell, "Delusions," *Millennial Harbinger*, 2 (February 1831), 91.

2. Smith, *History of the Church*, Vol. IV, p. 461.

3. Joseph Smith Jr., *The Book of Mormon* (Palmyra, New York: Egbert E. Grandin, 1830), title page.

4. Joseph Smith Jr., *Book of Mormon* (Salt Lake City: Corporation of the President of the Church of Jesus Christ of Latter-day Saints, 1981), 2.

5. *Journal of Discourses* (Liverpool: F.D. Richards, Latter-day Saints' Book Depot, 1854), Vol. 7, pp. 114-115.

6. Smith, *History of the Church*, Vol. III, p. 232.

7. Smith, *Book of Mormon*, 2.

8. Smith, *Doctrine and Covenants*, 28:11.

9. Brodie, *No Man Knows My History*, 79.

10. *Brigham Young University Travel Study Update* (Provo, Utah: Brigham Young University), Winter, 1990.

11. Hugh Nibley, *An Approach to the Book of Mormon* (Salt Lake City: Deseret News Press, 1964), 3.

12. Quoted in Walter Martin, *Kingdom of the Cults* (Minneapolis: Bethany House Publishers, 1985), 184.

13. Department of Anthropology, The Smithsonian Institution, *Statement Regarding the Book of Mormon* (Washington: National Museum of Natural History, Spring 1987), 1-2.

14. Smith, *History of the Church*, Vol. IV, p. 461.

15. Merrill Unger, *Archaeology and the Old Testament* (Chicago: Moody Press, 1954), 15.

16. M.T. Lamb, *The Golden Bible, or, The Book of Mormon, Is It from God?* (New York: Ward & Drummond, 1887), 89-90.

17. Hoekema, *Mormonism*, 83.

18. Marvin Cowan, *Mormon Claims Answered* (By the author, 1975), 52.

19. Campbell, "Delusions," 95.

20. Smith, *History of the Church*, Vol. IV, p. 461.

Chapter 3

Smith's Other Works

In addition to the *Book of Mormon*, Joseph Smith, Jr. is primarily responsible for two other volumes, *Doctrine and Covenants* and *Pearl of Great Price*. These, along with the *Book of Mormon* and the Bible, make up what Mormons call their "four standard works." Contrary to claims of Mormons, the Bible is not viewed as equal to the other three but is instead considered to be an inferior source of truth. That is because it is seen as fraught with error. Joseph Smith said, "I believe the Bible as it read when it came from the pen of the original writers. Ignorant translators, careless transcribers, or designing and corrupt priests have committed many errors."[1]

In this section, *Doctrine and Covenants* and *Pearl of Great Price*, as well as a third effort at translating what has become known as the Kinderhook Plates, will be considered.

Doctrine and Covenants

Doctrine and Covenants, first published in its current form in 1876, contains 136 sections each of which is divided into verses. All the sections except 136 contain revelations supposedly given through Joseph Smith. Section 136 was purportedly revealed through Brigham Young. The present edition of *Doctrine and Covenants* also contains the "Manifesto" prohibiting polygamy issued by President Wilford Woodruff in 1890. The various "revelations" of *Doctrine and Covenants* deal with such subjects as the church, God's nature, the priesthood, the millennium, the resurrection, the state of man after death and the various grades of salvation. Many of these "revelations" are addressed to specific individuals.

Section 19, for example, is addressed to Martin Harris and commands him to "pay the debt thou hast contracted with the printer" (v. 35). In Section 104 a revelation is given directing the distribution of some lots and houses in Kirtland, Ohio (vv. 20-46). In Section 132, the well known section on plural marriage, an "oracle" is addressed to Emma Smith, Joseph's wife, telling her that she must stand ready to receive additional wives that have been given to her husband or suffer eternal destruction (vv. 52-54). *Doctrine and Covenants* deals with baptism for the dead, celestial marriage and polygamy. It is actually more relevant to Mormonism than the *Book of Mormon* itself, as it contains much more doctrinal material.[2] The RLDS group rejects portions of *Doctrine and Covenants*, including parts dealing with polygamy.

Pearl of Great Price

The *Pearl of Great Price* is much smaller than *Doctrine and Covenants*. Included in it is, first of all, the Book of Moses, a work of eight chapters covering the same general period as that covered by the first six chapters of Genesis. This book is a copy of the opening chapters of Smith's *Inspired Version* of the Bible. Next is the Book of Abraham, purporting to be a translation from an Egyptian papyrus. This book, supposedly written by Abraham while in Egypt, tells about Kolob, which is said to be the greatest of all the stars and the one nearest to God. It discusses the pre-existence of souls, the plan to prepare an earth for those souls, the plan to subject those souls to a period of probation on earth, and the organization of matter by which the heavens and the earth were formed.[3]

The *Pearl of Great Price* contains Joseph Smith's translation of Matthew 24. It also has excerpts from *History of Joseph Smith, the Prophet*—the section of Smith's autobiography which narrates the discovery of the plates and their translation. Finally in the *Pearl*, we find the Articles of Faith, which is a body of doctrinal information considered very important to Mormons today.

No part of the *Pearl of Great Price* has been more scrutinized by non-Mormons and proved to be more of an embarrassment to the Mormon church than the Book of Abraham. In the early 1830s, an Englishman acquired some Egyptian mummies which became the property of his nephew, Michael Chandler. Chandler, who decided to travel throughout the United States showing these mummies for money, opened an exhibit in Kirtland, Ohio, on July 3, 1835, where the majority of Mormons were settled at that time.[4]

Smith purchased the mummies and accompanying papyri. Upon examination, he declared that one papyrus contained the writings of Abraham while in Egypt, and another was the work of Joseph, son of Jacob. Smith proceeded to "translate" a portion of a papyrus. The translation was first published in 1842 in the church's paper, *Times and Seasons*. The Book of Abraham is accompanied in the *Pearl of Great Price* by three drawings from the papyri.

For years, Mormons looked upon the Book of Abraham as a potential opportunity to verify Smith's translating ability. That is true because the plates for the *Book of Mormon* were supposedly returned to God, and could not be used for verification. Smith reportedly translated the Book of Abraham with the Urim and Thummim, the same instruments he claimed to use in the translation of the *Book of Mormon*.

Numerous Egyptologists examined the drawings from the Egyptian papyri reproduced in the Book of Abraham and compared them with Smith's accompanying translation. They concluded that the scrolls were simply papyri commonly buried with mummies containing instructions for the afterlife. Not one Egyptologist found the papyri had anything even remotely to do with Abraham (in his "translation" work, Smith got 1,125 words from 46 characters). Up until a few years ago, Egyptologists had only Mormon drawings to evaluate.

In 1967 the original papyri, long thought to have been destroyed by the Chicago fire, were found and presented to the Mormon church. A number of Egyptologists have evaluated the original documents and have unanimously agreed with the previous conclusion—Joseph Smith's "translation" was no translation at all. One researcher said, referring to Joseph's work on one of the documents, "If anything could be more destructive to Smith's claim to 'understand the Egyptian language as practiced by the ancients,' it is found in the fact that Joseph even translated the holes in the papyrus."[5]

Dr. Hugh Nibley, whom the Mormons consider their foremost authority on the Egyptian language, commented, "The papyri scripts given to the church do not prove the Book of Abraham is true....LDS scholars are caught flat footed by this discovery."[6]

The Kinderhook Plates

In 1843 an incident occurred which has proven to be a great embarrassment to the Mormon church. Three men, Bridge Whitton, Robert Wiley, and Wilbur Fugate, made six metal plates and etched Chinese characters on them with acid. They then rusted the plates to give them an aged appearance and buried them along with some Indian bones. Wiley spread the word that he had dreamed three nights in a row about buried treasure, and invited help in finding it. Mormons were present at the unearthing of the plates. When the plates were brought to Smith, he wrote in his journal, "I have translated a portion of them, and found they contain the history of the person with which they were found. He was a descendant of Ham, through the loins of Pharaoh, king of Egypt, and that he received his kingdom from the ruler of heaven and earth."[7]

One plate is still in existence and has been examined by several modern scientists. They have concluded that the composition and construction identify the plate as a product of a blacksmith shop of the 1840s. According to scientific analysis, the inscriptions could indeed have been made with acid, and are inscribed with symbols likely copied from a Chinese tea box.[8]

Notes

1. Joseph Smith, Jr., *Teachings of the Prophet Joseph Smith*, selected and arranged by Joseph Fielding Smith (Salt Lake City: Deseret Book Co., 1958), 327.

2. Hoekema, *Mormonism*, 30.

3. Ibid., 30-31.

4. John A. Wilson, *Signs and Wonders upon Pharaoh* (Chicago: University of Chicago Press, 1964), 37.

5. Wesley P. Walters, *Joseph Smith Among the Egyptians* (Salt Lake City: Utah Lighthouse Ministry, 1973), reprint, *Journal of the Evangelical Theological Society*, 16 (Winter 1973), 43.

6. *Daily Universe*, "Brigham Young University," Dec. 1, 1967, as quoted by Tanner, *Mormonism—Shadow or Reality*, 294, 298.

7. Smith, *History of the Church*, Vol. V, p. 372.

8. Latayne Colvett Scott, *The Mormon Mirage* (Grand Rapids: Zondervan Publishing House, 1979), 49.

Chapter 4

Doctrines of Mormonism

The apostle Paul wrote in 2 Corinthians 11:3, "But I fear, lest by any means, as the serpent beguiled Eve through his subtilty, so your minds should be corrupted from the simplicity that is in Christ." Clearly, the Bible teaches that truth by nature is straightforward. What has been considered about Mormonism thus far, however, suggests not simplicity but a complex web of dogma. Indeed, Mormon doctrine is confusing and constantly changing. It appears that Joseph Smith, Jr. had difficulty deciding just what the teachings of his church would be. Likewise, Smith's successors have shown little reluctance to refashion the doctrine of the Latter-day Saints when convenient.

Changes in so-called revelation began very early in Mormon history. David Whitmer was one of the three original witnesses to the *Book of Mormon*. He, along with his two comrades, grew disenchanted with the Mormon faith. Whitmer wrote that Sidney Rigdon, a very influential leader in the early days of the movement,

> ...was a thorough Bible scholar, a man of fine education, and a powerful orator. He soon worked himself deep into Brother

Joseph's affections, and had more influence over him than any other man living....Brother Joseph rejoiced, believing that the Lord had sent him this great and mighty man....Poor Brother Joseph! He was mistaken about this...Sidney Rigdon was the cause of almost all the errors which were introduced while he was in the church. Rigdon would expound the Old Testament scriptures of the Bible and *Book of Mormon* (in his way) to Joseph,...and would persuade Brother Joseph to inquire of the Lord about this doctrine and that doctrine, and of course a revelation would always come just as they desired it.[1]

The attitudes of Smith and Rigdon toward Mormon doctrine typify LDS thinking from its earliest days until now. The unstable and confusing nature of Mormonism is evident from an examination of the following doctrines.

Doctrine of Continuous Revelation

Mormons believe that divine revelation is continuous; that is, since God spoke with men in Bible times he must do so in the same way today. Latter-day Saints believe that applies even in the case of written revelation. *Doctrine and Covenants* 68:4 says, referring to Mormon leaders, "And whatsoever they shall speak when moved upon by the Holy Ghost shall be scripture, shall be the will of the Lord, shall be the mind of the Lord, shall be the word of the Lord, shall be the voice of the Lord, and the power of God unto salvation." Likewise Brigham Young declared:

I will make a statement here that has been brought against me as a crime, perhaps, or as any fault in my life...—that Brigham Young has said "when he sends forth his discourses to the world they may call them Scripture." I say now, when they are copied and approved by me they are as good Scripture as is couched in this Bible, and if you want to read revelation read the sayings of him who knows the mind of God.[2]

The Mormon church is not only founded upon the *Book of Mormon* but has also produced *Doctrine and Covenants* and *Pearl of Great Price*. Since its establishment, a steady stream of so-called revelations has been generated—some directly contradicting others.

A classic example of the inconsistencies that have resulted from continuous revelations is the doctrine of polygamy. Joseph Smith and Brigham Young commanded the practice.[3] In *Doctrine and Covenants* 132:1 Smith states:

> Verily thus saith the Lord unto you my servant Joseph, that inasmuch as you have inquired of my hand to know and understand wherein I, the Lord, justified my servants Abraham, Isaac, and Jacob, as also Moses, David and Solomon, my servants, as touching the principle and doctrine of their having many wives and concubines.

One author, in italicizing the word "justified," accurately observes, "Thus, with no prefatory argument, Joseph Smith resolved for the Mormon mind the question of whether or not God approved of the Old Testament practice of plural marriage. Joseph bypassed the whole issue by saying that not only did God tolerate it, but that he required it."[4]

It is interesting that while Smith convinced many early Mormons to embrace the practice, he was not successful in persuading his wife. In a futile effort to bring her around to his way of thinking, Smith produced a special revelation, now recorded in *Doctrine and Covenants* section 132:

> And let mine handmaid, Emma Smith, receive all those that have been given unto my servant Joseph, and who are virtuous and pure before me; and those who are not pure, and have said they were pure, shall be destroyed, saith the Lord God....—if any man espouse a virgin, and desire to espouse another, and the first give her consent, and if he espouse the second, and they are virgins, and have vowed to no other man, then is he justified; he cannot commit adultery....if he have ten virgins given unto him by this law, he cannot commit adultery, for they belong to him, and they are given unto him; therefore is he justified.[5]

Polygamy was rescinded by Wilford Woodruff, a later president of the Mormon church, in 1890.[6] Both the practice of polygamy and its discontinuation are commanded in *Doctrine and Covenants*.

Brigham Young taught that Adam was God. He called Adam "Michael, the Archangel, the Ancient of Days."[7] Spencer W. Kimball, a recent president, reversed Young's revelation and labeled the Adam-God doctrine as false teaching. These and many other examples indicate that a study of the faith of the Latter-day Saints is a study of continuing, conflicting, contradicting revelation. If God is still causing men to write Scriptures as he did in New Testament times, there must still be, it stands to reason, apostles and prophets to deliver fresh, new insights. Herein lies the logic behind those offices in the Mormon church.

Perhaps a clue to understanding why Mormons feel comfortable with contradictions in their so-called revelations is found in a comment made by David Whitmer in his work, *An Address to All Believers in Christ*. Whitmer, as previously noted, was one of the three original witnesses to the *Book of Mormon*. He quit the Mormon church and produced that work as an exposé of the religion. Whitmer wrote:

> When the *Book of Mormon* was in the hands of the printer, more money was needed to finish the printing of it....Brother Hyrum said it had been suggested to him that some of the brethren might go to Toronto, Canada, and sell the copy-right of the *Book of Mormon* for considerable money: and he persuaded Joseph to inquire of the Lord about it. Joseph concluded to do so. He...received a revelation that some of the brethren should go to Toronto, Canada, and that they would sell the copy-right of the *Book of Mormon*. Hiram Page and Oliver Cowdery went to Toronto on this mission, but they failed entirely to sell the copyright, returning without any money. Joseph was at my father's house when they returned. I was there also, and am an eye witness to these facts....Well, we were all in great trouble, and we asked Joseph how it was that he had received a revelation from the Lord for some brethren to go to Toronto and sell the copy-right, and the brethren had utterly failed in their undertaking. Joseph did not know how it was, so he enquired of the Lord about it, and behold

the following revelation came through the stone: "Some revelations are of God: some revelations are of man: and some revelations are of the devil."[8]

Astonishingly, Smith himself admitted that some of his revelations were of Satan! One wonders how his followers knew which oracles were of God and which were of the devil. Obviously he asserted the revelation to go to Toronto and sell the copyright was of God until it didn't work out. How could anyone (including Smith) know whether or not the *Book of Mormon* was of God or the devil? And what about the *Pearl of Great Price* and *Doctrine and Covenants*?

Unfortunately for Mormonism, the Bible does not teach that revelation is continuous. Hebrews 1:1-2 states, "God, who at sundry times and in divers manners spake in time past unto the fathers by the prophets, hath in these last days spoken unto us by his Son, whom he hath appointed heir of all things, by whom also he made the worlds."

Christ is the spokesman for the last days and he did his speaking through the New Testament, both by his own words and those of his inspired apostles. The Bible plainly teaches, then, that the Scriptures revealed in its pages give humanity all necessary truth. In 2 Timothy 3:16-17 the Word of God says, "All scripture is given by inspiration of God, and is profitable for doctrine, for reproof, for correction, for instruction in righteousness: that the man of God may be perfect, thoroughly furnished unto all good works."

James expressed the finality and completeness of the New Testament in this manner: "But whoso looketh into the perfect law of liberty, and continueth therein, he being not a forgetful hearer, but a doer of the work, this man shall be blessed in his deed" (James 1:25). By referring to the New Testament as "perfect," the passage tells us first that it has no room for improvement. Secondly, it is complete, since perfection implies completeness. The original Greek term for "perfect" in this passage is *teleion*, which means "having

reached its end, finished, complete, perfect."[9] Unquestionably, the wording of James rules out further periods of revelation.

One of the most decisive declarations of the finality of
Biblical revelation is found in 1 Corinthians 13:8-13, where
the Bible states:

> Charity never faileth: but whether there be prophecies, they shall
> fail; whether there be tongues, they shall cease; whether there be
> knowledge, it shall vanish away. For we know in part, and we
> prophesy in part. But when that which is perfect is come, then
> that which is in part shall be done away. When I was a child, I
> spake as a child, I understood as a child, I thought as a child: but
> when I became a man, I put away childish things. For now we see
> through a glass, darkly; but then face to face: now I know in part;
> but then shall I know even as also I am known. And now abideth
> faith, hope, charity, these three; but the greatest of these is charity.

In this passage the apostle Paul predicted the end of
miraculous gifts. They would conclude, he wrote, when "that
which is perfect" came. The "perfect" is the perfect law of
liberty (James 1:25), or the New Testament, as previously
noticed. Upon completion of the New Testament, miraculous
endowments ceased. Specifically mentioned is the gift of
prophecy (1 Corinthians 13:8), which enabled men to reveal
God's will. Without that gift, revelation must came to a
screeching halt. Divine revelation is therefore not continuous
but was limited to the early years of Christianity.

Where does this leave us? Mormon claims to the contrary,
the Bible does not teach that there were two deliveries of the
faith, one in the Americas and one in Bible lands. In Jude 3
the Word of God exhorts us to "earnestly contend for the
faith which was once delivered unto the saints." Jude plainly
declares there was only one delivery—in Palestine 1900
years ago.

It cannot be overemphasized that the doctrine of continuous revelation is the very foundation of the Church of Jesus

Christ of Latter-day Saints. All the beliefs which distinguish the Mormon faith from Christianity are the result of alleged modern-day prophets and their writings. The very concept of a contemporary stream of information from God crumbles in light of the Bible.

Doctrine of God

Latter-day Saints teach a unique doctrine of God. Mormonism began as a monotheistic, Trinitarian religion. In fact, the *Book of Mormon* presents a basically Biblical view of God. In 2 Nephi 31:21 the volume says, "And now, behold, this is the doctrine of Christ, and the only and true doctrine of the Father, and of the Son and of the Holy Ghost, which is one God, without end." Alma 11:26-29 also declares, "And Zeezrom said unto him, 'Thou sayest that there is a true and living God?' And Amulek said: 'Yea, there is a true and living God.' Now Zeezrom said, 'Is there more than one God?' And he answered, 'No.'"

Likewise, the "Testimony of Three Witnesses" at the beginning of the *Book of Mormon* teaches the oneness of God, stating, "And honor be to the Father, and to the Son, and to the Holy Ghost, which is one God." According to Alma 18:28, God is a spirit being: "This Great Spirit, who is God, created all things."

Mormonism teaches polytheism. Soon after the founding of his church, Joseph Smith began to develop theories about God's nature which would soon become the basis for the Mormon understanding of Deity. Consequently, Mormons teach polytheism. Both Smith and Brigham Young affirmed that three separate gods, named Elohim, Jehovah, and Michael, collaborated in organizing and populating the earth. Had they read their Bibles more, Brigham and Joseph would have known that Jehovah and Elohim are different names for the same person.

With his multiple-deity concept in mind, Joseph Smith said, "In the beginning the head of the Gods called a council of the Gods; and they came together and concocted a plan to create the world and people it."[10] Additionally, Abraham 4:1 declares, "And then the Lord said: Let us go down. And they went down at the beginning, and they, that is the Gods, organized and formed the heavens and the earth." Brigham Young stated, "How many gods there are, I do not know."[11]

A surprising facet of Mormon polytheism is the teaching that there is a heavenly mother, a doctrine which has decided Roman Catholic overtones. Mormon apostle Bruce Mc-Conkie wrote, "Implicit in the Christian verity that all men are the spirit children of an Eternal Father is the usually unspoken truth that they are also the offspring of an Eternal Mother."[12]

Polytheism is one of the most serious heresies of Mormonism. Judeo-Christian religion is built on the foundation of one true God. The Bible firmly insists that God is one. Jeremiah 10:10-11 declares:

> But the Lord is the true God, he is the living God, and an everlasting king: at his wrath the earth shall tremble, and the nations shall not be able to abide his indignation. Thus shall ye say unto them, The gods that have not made the heavens and the earth, even they shall perish from the earth, and from under these heavens.

Isaiah likewise uttered the words of God, saying, "...ye may know and believe me, and understand that I am he: before me there was no God formed, neither shall there be after me" (Isaiah 43:10). Jesus declared in Mark 12:29, "The Lord our God is one Lord." Ephesians 4:6 states that there is "one God and Father of all, who is above all and through all and in you all." In 1 Timothy 1:17, the Bible refers to "the King eternal, immortal, invisible, the only wise God." In 1 Timothy 6:15-16 the Bible describes God as "the King of kings, and Lord of lords; who only hath immortality, dwelling in light which no man can approach unto; whom no man hath seen, nor can see." If God had wanted to make plainer the truth that he is one, it is difficult to imagine what additional words could have been used.

Mormons teach that God has a physical body. In *Doctrine and Covenants* 130:22, we read, "The Father has a body of flesh and bones as tangible as man's; the Son also; but the Holy Ghost has not a body of flesh and bones, but is a personage of Spirit." Mormons teach that mankind was *physically* created in God's image. In the Book of Moses 6:9, a part of *Pearl of Great Price*, we read, "In the image of his own body, male and female, created he them." According to *Principles of the Gospel*, "Our bodies are patterned after his, and in the resurrection we will receive perfected, immortal bodies, just as he has."[13]

Early Mormon apostle Parley P. Pratt wrote, "...each of these Gods, including Jesus Christ and his Father, being in possession of not merely an organized spirit but also a glorious immortal body of flesh and bones."[14] Pratt further indicated that an invisible god is less powerful than pagan idols:

> There never has been a visible idol worshipped among men that was so powerless as this "God without body, parts, or passions." The god of Egypt, the crocodile, could destroy. The images of different nations could be felt and seen. The Peruvian god, the sun, could diffuse its genial warmth, light and influence. But not so with the God without "body, parts, or passions." That which has no parts has no whole. Beings that have no passions have no soul.[15]

The Bible teaches that God does not have a physical body. In 1 John 4:12, the Bible says, "If we love one another, God dwelleth in us." Dwelling in each believer would be rather difficult for a deity with a body of flesh. Jeremiah further recorded, "Am I a God at hand, saith the Lord, and not a God afar off? Can any hide himself in secret places that

I shall not see him? saith the Lord. Do I not fill heaven and earth? saith the Lord" (Jeremiah 23:23-24).

Jeremiah there reveals that the God of the Bible is omnipresent (everywhere at the same time), an impossibility for a god of flesh. Paul wrote that Christ "is the image of the invisible God, the firstborn of every creature." That a fleshly god who both looks like a human and is invisible is absurd.

Again, John 4:24 says that "God is a Spirit." In Luke 24:39 Jesus said, "A spirit hath not flesh and bones." Let this be viewed logically:

        1. Since God is a Spirit, and
        2. A spirit hath not flesh and bones, then
        3. God hath not flesh and bones.

The doctrine that God has a physical body is false. Mormons, with this doctrine, have repeated the error of early pagans who completely rejected God. Those idolaters are described in Romans 1:22-23: "Professing themselves to be wise, they became fools, And changed the glory of the uncorruptible God into an image made like to corruptible man."

Mormons teach that God is progressive. Mormons teach that God has advanced from being a human to his current state. Early Mormon apostle Orson Hyde said, "Remember that God, our heavenly Father, was perhaps once a child, and mortal like we ourselves, and rose step by step in the scale of progress, in the school of advancement; has moved forward and overcome, until He has arrived at the point where He now is."[16] Furthermore, according to Joseph Smith in *Journal of Discourses*, "God himself is increasing and progressing in knowledge, power, and dominion, and will do so worlds without end."[17]

If it were true that God had advanced from being simply a human to a divine being, it would follow that other people could likewise progress to godhood. Mormons teach that to be the case. In fact, they carry the theory to its logical conclusion of a hierarchy of gods at different levels of development. Bruce McConkie wrote, "Hence, if Jesus had a father, can we not believe that *he* had a father also?" He wrote in the same context, that "there is an infinite number of holy personages, drawn from worlds without number, who have passed on to exaltation and are thus gods."[18]

The Bible teaches that God is not progressive. Psalm 102:27 states, "But thou art the same, and thy years shall have no end." In Malachi 3:6, God says, "For I am the Lord, I change not." While the Bible decisively refutes the false doctrine of divine progression, it needn't even be opened to find a successful argument against the tenet. The *Book of Mormon* itself thoroughly refutes it. In Mormon 9:9-10, 19, a book within the *Book of Mormon*, two New Testament passages are quoted which deal with the unchanging nature of God, Hebrews 13:8 and James 1:17. That volume says:

> For do we not read that God is the same yesterday, today, and forever, and in him there is no variableness neither shadow of changing? And now if ye have imagined up unto yourselves a god who doth vary, and in whom there is shadow of changing, then ye have imagined up unto yourselves a god who is not a God of miracles....I say unto you he changeth not; if so he would cease to be God.

Moroni 8:18 states, "For I know that God is not a partial God, neither a changeable being; but he is unchangeable from all eternity to all eternity" Likewise a passage in *Doctrine and Covenants* strongly refutes the notion that God is progressive and has developed from a human state.

> By these things we know that there is a God in heaven, who is infinite and eternal, from everlasting to everlasting the same unchangeable God, the framer of heaven and earth,...[He] gave unto them commandments that they should love and serve him, the only living and true God.[19]

Mormonism teaches that God, with a physical body, fathered Jesus Christ. Incredibly enough, Brigham Young stated, "When the Virgin Mary conceived the child Jesus, the Father had begotten him in his own likeness. He was *not* begotten by the Holy Ghost. And who is the Father? He is the first of the human family."[20] He again asserted, "When the time came that His first-born, the Savior, should come into the world and take a tabernacle, the Father came himself and favoured that spirit with a tabernacle instead of letting any *other* man do it [italics added]."[21] Young further taught, "The birth of the Savior was as natural as are the births of our children; it was the result of natural action. He partook of flesh and blood—was begotten of his Father, as we are of our fathers."[22]

The idea that the Messiah was begotten by literal intercourse is repugnant to every Christian. Scripture teaches that Jesus was miraculously conceived, not by a fleshly God, but by the Holy Spirit during which time Mary remained a virgin. In Matthew 1:18-23 the Bible says:

> Now the birth of Jesus Christ was on this wise: When as his mother Mary was espoused to Joseph, before they came together, she was found with child of the Holy Ghost. Then Joseph her husband, being a just man, and not willing to make her a publick example, was minded to put her away privily. But while he thought on these things, behold, the angel of the Lord appeared unto him in a dream, saying, Joseph, thou son of David, fear not to take unto thee Mary thy wife: for that which is conceived in her is of the Holy Ghost. And she shall bring forth a son, and thou shalt call his name JESUS: for he shall save his people from their sins. Now all this was done, that it might be fulfilled which was spoken of the Lord by the prophet, saying, Behold, a virgin shall be with child, and shall bring forth a son, and they shall call his name Emmanuel, which being interpreted is, God with us.

Mormonism has taught that Adam is God. This must rank as one of the most bizarre, confusing doctrines of the entire Latter-day Saint system of belief. Brigham Young stated:

> When our father Adam came into the garden of Eden, he came into it with a *celestial body,* and brought Eve, *one of his wives,* with him. He helped to make and organize this world. He is MICHAEL, the *Archangel,* the ANCIENT OF DAYS! about whom holy men have written and spoken—HE is our FATHER *and our* GOD, *and the only God with whom we have to do.* Every man upon the earth, professing Christians or non-professing, must hear it, and *will know it sooner or later.*[23]

Mormon Apostle Orson Pratt is among the many LDS voices from the past reaffirming the doctrine. He wrote, "Every knee shall bow, and every tongue confess that he is the God of the whole earth. Then will the words of the Prophet Brigham, when speaking of Adam, be fully realized—'He is our father and our God, and the only God with whom we have to do.'"[24]

That doctrine is today an embarrassment to the Mormon church, and some have claimed, contrary to overwhelming evidence, that it was never taught. Mormon apostle Bruce McConkie has acknowledged that no less than Young taught the doctrine, and has labeled Young's teaching as false. In a letter to Mr. Eugene England dated February 19, 1981, McConkie wrote, referring to a devotional held at Brigham Young University:

> In that same devotional speech I said, "There are those who believe or say they believe that Adam is our father and our God, that he is the father of our spirits and our bodies, and that he is the one we worship." I, of course, indicated the utter absurdity of this doctrine and said it was totally false....Cultists...have expounded upon the views of Brigham Young and others of the early Brethren relative to Adam. They have plain and clear quotations saying all of the things about Adam which I say are false. The quotations are in our literature.[25]

McConkie and other Mormons who have earmarked the doctrine as false raise a serious question. Brigham Young was supposedly a prophet. In fact, he declared that to be the case and it was recognized and accepted by the millions in the Utah church who followed him faithfully. Young said his pronouncements were "as good Scripture as is couched in this Bible, and if you want to read revelation read the sayings of him who knows the mind of God."[26]

Either Brigham Young taught false doctrine or he didn't. Either his teachings were revealed truth or they weren't. If Young erred in the Adam-God doctrine, how can Mormons know if he taught truth on anything else? How can they know whether he represented God or Satan in his doctrines? Simply speaking, they cannot know. If Young can present a doctrine as true which is actually false, how can Mormons know that Joseph Smith, and all other LDS prophets didn't do the same thing?

According to Mormon teaching, someone of the stature of Brigham Young can disseminate false doctrine. Perhaps, by that reasoning, all the Mormon prophets have taught falsely. If Young taught one false doctrine, how can anyone be sure that all his teachings are not false? How can anyone be sure that *all* the teachings of *all* Latter-day Saint prophets are not likewise false? These are some questions that Mormonism cannot answer.

In labeling the Adam-God doctrine as false, Mr. McConkie was correct. The Bible explicitly teaches that Adam was not divine but a mere mortal created by God who lived and died like other humans. In Genesis 5:5 the Bible says, "And all the days that Adam lived were 930 years: and he died." God absolutely eliminated the possibility of his having evolved from Adam by declaring in Malachi 3:6, "For I am the Lord, I change not." In Numbers 23:19, the Adam-God theory is thoroughly refuted: "God is not a man, that he should lie; neither the son of man, that he should repent."

Doctrine of Christ

Mormonism teaches several bizarre doctrines concerning Jesus Christ. In fact, the Mormon concept of Christ is so far from the Bible picture that in no sense can the LDS faith be called a "Christian" religion.

It is taught that Christ has no unique attributes that cannot be acquired by others as they progress spiritually. This is consistent with the previously cited doctrine that God is merely an exalted man. Parley Pratt wrote, "Every man who is eventually made perfect—raised from the dead and filled, or quickened, with a fullness of celestial glory—will become like them [Christ and God the Father] in every respect, physically and in intellect, attributes and powers.[27]

The Bible, to the contrary, teaches that Christ is Deity. In John 1:1, 14, the Bible says, "In the beginning was the Word, and the Word was with God, and the Word was God. And the word was made flesh, and dwelt among us, (and we beheld his glory, the glory as of the only begotten of the Father) full of grace and truth." He is more than the first of many like creatures to be born; he is actually part of the Godhead. The Bible says, "For in him dwelleth all the fulness of the God-head bodily" (Colossians 2:9). Christ was not the first born of all preexistent souls, as Mormons teach, but has always existed. He declared, "Before Abraham was, I am" (John 8:58).

Jesus' earthly life was absolutely sinless. In 1 Peter 2:22 the Bible says that he "did no sin, neither was guile found in his mouth." We humans, on the other hand, are all guilty of sin. John wrote, "If we say that we have no sin, we deceive ourselves, and the truth is not in us" (1 John 1:8). That men are not of the same nature as Christ is proven by Acts 4:12, where Peter preached, "Neither is there salvation in any other: for there is none other name under heaven given among men, whereby we must be saved." Jesus, and Jesus alone is the one through whom salvation is dispensed.

Mormonism teaches that Christ was a polygamist. It is even asserted that he was married at the wedding at Cana of Galilee. Orson Hyde wrote, "Jesus was the bridegroom at the marriage of Cana of Galilee."[28] According to Mormon dogma, Christ was not only married but also had children. Hyde further taught, "Jesus Christ was married at Cana of Galilee....Mary, Martha and others were his wives, and...he begat children."[29]

This theory is blasphemously incorrect, since the Bible teaches that Christ's bride is the church. Ephesians 5:25, 31-32 declares:

> Husbands, love your wives, even as Christ also loved the church, and gave himself for it....For this cause shall a man leave his father and mother, and shall be joined unto his wife, and they two shall be one flesh. This is a great mystery; but I speak concerning Christ and the church.

Mormonism teaches that Satan and Jesus were spirit brothers and sons of God before Jesus was given a body. According to the Book of Moses, "Satan came among them, saying: I am also a son of God;...and they loved Satan more than God."[30] Christ is likewise identified as a son of God in Moses 4:1-4, which means that Satan and Christ are siblings. As has been pointed out, the fact that Christ is Deity precludes such a relationship. The Word of God teaches that Jesus is God's only Son. The Bible says, "For God so loved the world, that he gave his only begotten Son, that whosoever believeth in him should not perish, but have everlasting life" (John 3:16).

Doctrine of the Holy Spirit

Mormonism teaches a unique and confusing doctrine of the Holy Spirit. Bruce McConkie explains the Mormon view of the Spirit, though his explanation does not harmonize with all other Mormon writings on the subject:

> Three separate and distinct meanings of the title, Spirit of the Lord, are found in the revelations: 1. It has reference to the spirit body of Christ our Lord...; 2. It is used to mean the spirit of Jesus Christ, or light of truth, or light of Christ—the Spirit which is impersonal and fills the immensity of space, the Spirit which is the agency by means of which God governs and controls in all things; and 3. It is also a synonym for the Holy Ghost, that Spirit entity or personage of spirit who is a member of the Godhead.[31]

Clearly, the Mormons are under the misapprehension that there is a difference between the Spirit and the Holy Ghost. Mormons believe the Holy Ghost is a member of the Godhead, as we have seen, and that he is a person like the Father and the Son, except that he has a male spirit body instead of an actual physical body.[32] Because he has a spirit body, the Holy Ghost cannot be everywhere at once. He may visit men who are worthy, but he can't "tarry" with them.[33] The Holy Ghost is the personage given on Pentecost "after faith, repentance, and baptism."[34] Interestingly enough, the Holy Ghost, although a person, is referred to as "it" in Mormon writings.

Mormons see the Spirit of the Lord as an impersonal force found everywhere. They do not believe the Spirit is part of the Godhead. Mormon teaching is that the Spirit dwells in all good men, whereas the Holy Ghost guides only those who have obeyed the LDS gospel and have had hands laid upon them. The Bible teaches, however, that the words "spirit" and "ghost" are synonymous, both translated from the Greek word *pneuma*. In the Scriptures the terms are even used interchangeably in the same context. John 7:39 states, "But this he spake of the Spirit, which they that believe on him should receive: for the Holy Ghost was not yet given; because that Jesus was not yet glorified."

Doctrine of Man

Mormons believe that before men inhabited the earth, they existed as spirits. Joseph Smith asserted in a revelation given to the Mormon church on May 6, 1833, at Kirtland, Ohio, "Man was also in the beginning with God. Intelligence, or the light of truth, was not created or made, neither indeed can be. For man is spirit. The elements are eternal, and spirit and element, inseparably connected, receive a fullness of joy."[35]

Brigham Young elaborated on that concept, declaring, "Our Father in Heaven begat all the spirits that ever were, or ever will be, upon this earth and they were born spirits in the eternal world."[36] The theory that all humans existed before birth in a spirit world is now a bedrock doctrine of the LDS church. In fact, Mormon parents, as they have babies, believe they are providing bodies for these spirits. That's why they tend to have large families.

Mormons view the span of existence before birth as a probationary, schooling period—a concept which is at the root of Latter-day Saint racism. Bruce McConkie wrote:

> There is a reason why one man is born black and with other disadvantages, while another is born white with great advantages. The reason is that we once had an estate before we came here, and were obedient, more or less, to the laws that were given us there. Those who were faithful in all things there received greater blessings here, and those who were not faithful received less.[37]

The Bible teaches that men sprang from other humans— created beings—and were not "born" in any sense before their physical birth. Adam and Eve, the progenitors of the human race, were miraculously created. After them, all people were born naturally. Genesis 1:27-28 declares, "So God created man in his own image, in the image of God created he him; male and female created he them. And God blessed them, and God said unto them, be fruitful and multiply."

Mormonism teaches racism. While the above doctrine hints at the racial prejudice which undergirds the Mormon church, in other declarations extreme racial bias is much more obvious. Brigham Young reflected the raw bigotry of Mormonism when he wrote:

> You see some classes of the human family that are black, uncouth, uncomely, disagreeable and low in their habits, wild, and seemingly deprived of nearly all the blessings of the intelligence that is generally bestowed upon mankind....Cain slew his brother. Cain might have been killed, and that would have put a termination to that line of human beings. This was not to be, and the Lord put a mark upon him, which is the flat nose and black skin.[38]

Young further declared that interracial marriage with blacks is a sin so vile, it demands the death penalty. He stated, "Shall I tell you the law of God in regard to the African race? If the white man who belongs to the chosen seed mixes his blood with the seed of Cain, the penalty, under the law of God, is death on the spot. This will always be so."[39]

Those statements were typical of the Mormon attitude toward blacks until well into the middle twentieth century. In fact, Mormon dogma forbade blacks from occupying the priesthood until fairly recently. As the civil rights movement grew in strength, pressure increased upon the LDS church to rescind that discriminatory practice and other manifestations of prejudice. In the early seventies, several universities refused to engage in athletic and academic competition with Brigham Young University specifically because of the bigotry of the Latter-day Saints. Finally, on June 1, 1978, Mormon President Spencer W. Kimball received a "revelation" which authorized the ordaining of blacks to the priesthood.

Incidentally, Mormon writings do not merely indicate a prejudicial attitude toward blacks; we have already seen that the LDS view of the American Indian is based upon the presupposition that their dark skins indicate punishment from God.

While the Mormon faith nurtured and even elevated racism to the level of doctrine, Christianity distinguished itself from the beginning of its existence by a repudiation of racial boundaries. The Bible says, "God is no respecter of persons: but in every nation he that feareth him, and worketh righteousness, is accepted with him" (Acts 10:34-35). One of the reasons Christ died was to provide ground upon which all races could unite. Paul wrote:

> ...having abolished in his flesh the enmity, even the law of commandments contained in ordinances; for to make in himself of twain one new man; so making peace; And that he might reconcile both unto God in one body by the cross, having slain the enmity thereby [Ephesians 2:15-16].

The blessings of salvation offered through Jesus Christ are offered without regard to one's race, nationality, gender or even social standing. In Galatians 3:27-28 the apostle Paul wrote by inspiration, "For as many of you as have been baptized into Christ have put on Christ. There is neither Jew nor Greek, there is neither bond nor free, there is neither male nor female: for ye are all one in Christ Jesus."

Mormons believe, incredibly, that the fall of man was a good thing. The *Book of Mormon* in 2 Nephi 2:22-25, says:

> And now, behold, if Adam had not transgressed he would not have fallen, but he would have remained in the garden of Eden. And all things which were created must have remained in the same state in which they were after they were created; and they must have remained forever, and had no end. And they would have had no children; wherefore they would have remained in a state of innocence, having no joy, for they knew no misery; doing no good, for they knew no sin. But behold, all things have been done in the wisdom of him who knoweth all things. Adam fell that men might be; and men are, that they might have joy.

Likewise, in the Book of Moses we find the following:

> And in that day Adam blessed God and was filled, and began to prophesy concerning all the families of the earth, saying: Blessed

be the name of God, for because of my transgression my eyes are opened, and in this life I shall have joy, and again in the flesh I shall see God. And Eve, his wife, heard all these things and was glad, saying: Were it not for our transgression we never should have had seed, and never should have known good and evil, and the joy of our redemption, and the eternal life which God giveth unto all the obedient [5:10-11].

Consider what is being said in the above passages: if Adam and Eve had not sinned they would have had no joy—but Adam fell so that men could have joy! Adam is even pictured as blessing God for the "eye-opening" experience his sin provided! Mormon theologian Joseph Fielding Smith agreed that the transgression in the Garden of Eden was a positive event. He stated, "The fall of man came as a blessing in disguise, and it was the means of furthering the purposes of the Lord in the progress of man, rather than a means of hindering them."[40]

Such reasoning is more closely aligned to that of Satan than that of Christ. The devil enticed Eve to sin in the Garden of Eden by similarly portraying her impending fall as something positive. Referring to the forbidden fruit, he declared, "For God doth know that in the day you eat thereof, then your eyes shall be opened, and ye shall be as gods, knowing good and evil" (Genesis 3:5).

Adam and Eve, however, did not find the result of sin was simply a knowledge of good and evil. Their fall was instead a grave spiritual tragedy whose sweeping consequences included toil anguish, physical death and estrangement from God. Genesis declares in Chapter 3, verses 16-19:

Unto the woman he said, I will greatly multiply thy sorrow and thy conception; in sorrow thou shalt bring forth children; and thy desire shall be to thy husband, and he shall rule over thee. And unto Adam he said, Because thou hast hearkened unto the voice of thy wife, and hast eaten of the tree, of which I commanded thee, saying, Thou shalt not eat of it: cursed is the ground for thy sake; in sorrow shalt thou eat of it all the days of thy life; thorns also and thistles shall it bring forth to thee; and thou shalt eat the herb of the field; in the sweat of thy face shalt thou eat bread, till thou return unto the ground; for out of it wast thou taken: for dust thou art, and unto dust shalt thou return.

The fall of Adam and Eve was an adverse event of such far-reaching repercussions that it required the death of God's only begotten Son. In Romans 5:19, the Bible declares, "For as by one man's disobedience many were made sinners, so by the obedience of one shall many be made righteous."

Mormons believe that men can become Gods. In fact, Mormons strive for that goal. Joseph Smith taught the following in his famous King Follet discourse:

Here then, is eternal life—to know the only wise and true God; and you have got to learn how to be Gods yourselves, and to be kings and priests to God, the same as all Gods have done before you, namely by going from one small degree to another, and from a small capacity to a great one; from grace to grace, from exaltation to exaltation, until you attain to the resurrection of the dead, and are able to dwell in the everlasting burnings, and to sit in glory, as do those who sit enthroned in everlasting power.[41]

Brigham Young said, "Gods exist, and we had better strive to be prepared to be one with them." Lorenzo Snow, fifth president of the Mormon church, said, "As man is, God once was: as God is, man may become." In fact, Snow wrote a poem called "Man's Destiny" in which he delineated Mormon beliefs on this subject:

Still, tis no phantom that we trace
Man's ultimatum in life's race;
This royal path has long been trod
By righteous men, each now a God:

As Abra'am, Isaac, Jacob, too,
First babes, then men—to gods they grew.
As man now is, our God once was;
As now God is, so man may be,—
Which doth unfold man's destiny.[42]

That created, finite man could become infinite Deity is a logical absurdity. The Bible picture is not that by striving we can one day earn for ourselves a position as gods. The Bible picture is that by God's love, kindness, and mercy those who have been faithful are admitted into heaven to live with him. Matthew 25:34 teaches, "Then shall the King say unto them on his right hand, Come, ye blessed of my Father, inherit the kingdom prepared for you from the foundation of the world."

Doctrine of the Bible

Mormon apostle James Talmage wrote, "The Church of Jesus Christ of Latter-day Saints accepts the Holy Bible as the foremost of her standard works, first among the books which have been proclaimed as her written guides in faith and doctrine."[43]

Many, upon reading and hearing that and similar statements, have been led to believe that the Mormons look at the Bible in the same way as most religious people. Such pronouncements as Talmage's, however, when compared to other declarations in Mormon writings, are seen for what they are—empty rhetoric.

Mormons in practice do not consider the Bible the most important of their recognized religious documents. In fact, when contradictions arise between their so-called revelations and the Bible, the Bible's teachings are cast aside. To set the stage for dismissing inconvenient doctrines, Mormons claim that translations of the Bible are inaccurate. This will be discussed in more detail in the last chapter, but two LDS statements on this matter will now be considered. James Talmage continued:

> There will be, there can be, no absolutely reliable translation of these or other scriptures unless it be effected through the gift of translation, as one of the endowments of the Holy Ghost....Let the Bible then be read reverently and with prayerful care, the reader

ever seeking the light of the Spirit that he may discern between truth and the errors of men.[44]

Joseph Smith asserted, "Ignorant translators, careless transcribers, or designing and corrupt priests have committed many errors."[45]

As we have seen, the Bible represents itself as a perfect guide, the "perfect law of liberty" (James 1:25), the source of all we need in the way of spiritual guidance. Furthermore, God has providentially preserved his word accurately through the ages. The prophet Isaiah wrote, "The grass withereth, the flower fadeth: but the word of our God shall stand forever" (Isaiah 40:8).

Doctrine of Heaven

In *Doctrine and Covenants* 76, Joseph Smith taught that there are three degrees of heaven. The first of these is the celestial. Those enjoying that grade have glory like the sun. Its occupants are faithful Mormons. Next is the terrestrial, in which inhabitants enjoy a lesser glory, like that of the moon. They will receive inferior glory because, although good and honorable while on earth, such persons were blinded by the craftiness of men. Last is the telestial level, in which inhabitants enjoy a still lesser glory, like that of the stars. Occupants are the dishonest, liars, sorcerers, and whoremongers.

Mormons try to find a scriptural basis for this teaching in 1 Corinthians 15:39-42, which says,

> All flesh is not the same flesh: but there is one kind of flesh of men, another flesh of beasts, another of fishes, and another of birds. There are also celestial bodies, and bodies terrestrial: but the one glory of the celestial is one, and the glory of the terrestrial is another. There is one glory of the sun, and another glory of the moon, and another glory of the stars: for one star differeth from another star in glory. So also is the resurrection of the dead. It is sown in corruption; it is raised in incorruption.

That passage makes no reference to degrees of glory in heaven. It is simply saying, "Look around you; see that there are different kinds of bodies here on earth. Is it such an incredible thing that God, who can create all these different bodies, can give a new body to those that are raised to live with him? Now look up to heaven and see that heavenly bodies differ. If God can make heavenly bodies with different degrees of luminescence, is it so incredible that he can give you a new, glorious body on resurrection day?" The Mormon doctrine of heaven, then, has no support from the Bible.

Doctrine of Hell

When the Mormon church began, controversy burned among religious people over whether or not there was a hell. Orthodox Christianity taught that there was such a place which lasted forever, but claims by Universalists who advocated neither a hell nor a Satan began to be heard in New York state. The *Book of Mormon*, apparently responding to that controversy, teaches forthrightly that there is a hell and a devil. In 2 Nephi 28:22-23 a warning is sounded against one in ancient America who was purportedly teaching that hell does not exist:

> And behold, others he flattereth away, and telleth them there is no hell; and he saith unto them; I am no devil, for there is none—and thus he whispereth in their ears, until he grasps them with his awful chains,...and all that have been seized therewith must...go into the place prepared for them, even a lake of fire and brimstone, which is endless torment.

Alma 1 likewise tells of a false teacher who went about preaching error; in verse 4 we discover that he was a Universalist:

> And he also testified unto the people that all mankind should be saved at the last day, and that they need not fear nor tremble, but

that they might lift up their heads and rejoice; for the Lord had created all men, and had also redeemed all men; and, end the end, all men should have eternal life.

Within a year of the publication of the *Book of Mormon*, however, Smith changed his mind concerning hell, deciding that it was not eternal after all. In *Doctrine and Covenants* 19:6, he said in a revelation to Martin Harris, "Nevertheless, it is not written that there should be no end to this torment."

Presently, there are divided views among Mormons concerning hell, its nature and duration, yet it seems that most Mormons reject an everlasting hell. Brigham Young stated,

> The sectarian doctrine of final rewards and punishments is as strange to me as their bodiless, partless, and passionless God. Every man will receive according to the deeds done in the body, whether they be good or bad. All men, excepting those who sin against the Holy Ghost, who shed innocent blood or who consent thereto, will be saved in some kingdom; for in my father's house, says Jesus, there are many mansions.[46]

The Mormon doctrine that hell is not infinite is false because it directly opposes the teachings of the Bible. In the parable of the sheep and the goats, Christ, discussing their eternal destiny, declares, "And these shall go away into everlasting punishment; but the righteous into life eternal" (Matthew 25:46). It should be noted here that life and punishment are of the same duration. The Greek term *aionion* is translated both "everlasting" and "eternal" in the passage.

When the Bible says, "But the...murderers, and whoremongers, and sorcerers, and idolaters, and all liars, shall have their part in the lake which burneth with fire and brimstone: which is the second death" (Revelation 21:8), it is speaking of punishment that has no end. Considering the types of sin that result in being cast into that lake, one can easily imagine why the prospect of eternal torment made Joseph Smith and Brigham Young uncomfortable.

Doctrine of Baptism for the Dead

Mormonism teaches the doctrine of proxy baptism; that is, that one may be baptized in the place of another who has died. First taught by Joseph Smith in August of 1840, the rite was originally practiced on behalf of departed relatives. James Talmage associates it with the appearance of Elijah to Smith and Oliver Cowdery at the dedication of the Kirtland Temple on April 3, 1836.[47] Later, Joseph Smith stated in *Doctrine and Covenants:*

> Verily, thus saith the Lord unto you concerning your dead: When any of you are baptized for your dead, let there be a recorder, and let him be eye-witness of your baptisms; let him hear with his ears, that he may testify of a truth, saith the Lord.[48]

The doctrine of proxy baptism contradicts both the Bible and the *Book of Mormon. Doctrine and Covenants* 128:5 indicates that baptism for the dead is for those "who should die without a knowledge of the gospel." On the other hand, Moroni 8:22-23 appears to teach that those without a knowledge of the gospel are, like little children, not lost:

> For behold that all little children are alive in Christ, and also all they that are without the law. For the power of redemption cometh on all them that have no law; wherefore, he that is not condemned, or he that is under no condemnation, cannot repent; and unto such baptism availeth nothing—But it is mockery before God, denying the mercies of Christ, and power of his Holy Spirit, and putting trust in dead works.

In Mosiah 15:26, the *Book of Mormon* states categorically that those who have died in their sins cannot be saved on judgment day.

> But behold, and fear, and tremble before God, for ye ought to tremble; for the Lord redeemeth none such that rebel against him and die in their sins; yea, even all those that have perished in their sins ever since the world began, that have willfully rebelled against God, that have known the commandments of God, and

would not keep them; these are they that have no part in the first resurrection.

Alma 34:32-34 is even more pointed when it says:

For behold, this life is the time for men to prepare to meet God; yea, behold the day of this life is the day for men to perform their labors....behold, if we do not improve our time while in this life, then cometh the night of darkness wherein there can be no labor performed. Ye cannot say, when ye are brought to that awful crisis, that I will repent, that I will return to my God.

While various Bible passages are used to support the tenet of baptizing people on behalf of others who have died, Mormonism's favorite proof text is 1 Corinthians 15:29. The Bible there states, "Else what shall they do which are baptized for the dead, if the dead rise not at all? Why are they then baptized for the dead?" Does Paul in 1 Corinthians 15 teach proxy baptism?

The Word of God declares that some of its contents are "hard to be understood" (2 Peter 3:16), and this passage falls into that category. Peter goes on to say that it is these difficult passages "which they that are unlearned and unstable wrest, as they do also the other scriptures, unto their own destruction" (2 Peter 3:16). The use of 1 Corinthians 15 to support proxy baptism is not a proper application of the Bible. It is, instead, an unconscionable twisting of a difficult passage to support a man-made religious theory. The verse cannot be teaching proxy baptism, because, if it were, it would contradict other teachings of the New Testament, and "God is not the author of confusion" (1 Corinthians 14:33).

For example, the idea of proxy baptism contradicts the account of the rich man and Lazarus found in Luke 16:19-31, which clearly teaches that once dead, a sinner has no further opportunity to be saved. If proxy baptism were taught in 1 Corinthians 15:29, it would contradict 2 Corinthians 5:10, which says, "For we must all appear before the Judgement seat of Christ; that every one may receive the things done in his body, according to that he hath done, whether it be good or bad." Only deeds "done in the body" will be considered on judgment day. Even if one could be baptized by proxy after his death, such an baptism would be worthless.

The concept of substitute baptism contradicts Bible teachings that one must believe in and confess Christ in addition to being baptized in order to be saved (Romans 10:9-10; Acts 10:43; Acts 15:9; et al.). Obviously a dead man can't do a lot of confessing. Baptism places a man in fellowship with Christians and Christ. Galatians 3:26-27 says, "For ye are all the children of God by faith in Christ Jesus. For as many of you as have been baptized into Christ have put on Christ." It is difficult to see how those purposes of baptism can be accomplished for one who is deceased.

In context, Paul in 1 Corinthians 15 is discussing the resurrection of the dead. He points out that if there is no resurrection Christian faith is vain (1 Corinthians 15:13-18). The apostle by inspiration discusses the order of the resurrection (1 Corinthians 15:23-24). He then points out that it is because of the resurrection that he has permitted himself to be persecuted (1 Corinthians 15:31-32). In this context he asks, "Else what shall they do which are baptized for the dead, if the dead rise not at all? why are they then baptized for the dead?" In other words, why are Christians baptized in preparation for their death? If the dead are not raised, what is the point of it? Proxy baptism is not even under discussion in this chapter or, for that matter, anywhere else in the Bible.

Mormons combine the fallacy of baptism for the dead with the error of obsessive interest in genealogy. Mormon apostle Bruce R. McConkie wrote:

Before vicarious ordinances of salvation and exaltation may be performed for those who have died without a knowledge of the gospel, but who presumably would have received it had the opportunity come to them, they must be accurately and properly identified. Hence, genealogical research is required. To aid its members in intelligent and effective research, the Church maintains in Salt Lake City one of the world's greatest genealogical societies.

The genealogical society literally contains "hundreds of millions of names."[49]

Such emphasis on genealogies is in direct violation of the Bible. We are admonished in 1 Timothy 1:4, "Neither give heed to fables and endless genealogies, which minister questions, rather than godly edifying which is in faith: so do." Again, Titus 3:9 commands, "But avoid foolish questions, and genealogies, and contentions, and strivings about the law; for they are unprofitable and vain."

Doctrine of the Priesthood

Mormonism teaches that physical priesthood was a part of primitive Christianity lost in apostasy. Mormon apostle James E. Talmage wrote:

> In the first ten centuries immediately following the ministry of Christ the authority of the Holy Priesthood was lost from among men, and no human power could restore it. But the Lord in his mercy provided for the reestablishment of His Church in the last days, and for the last time; and the prophets of olden time foresaw this era of renewed enlightenment, and sang in joyous tones of its coming. This restoration was effected by the Lord through the Prophet Joseph Smith, who, together with Oliver Cowdery, in 1829, received the Aaronic priesthood under the hands of John the Baptist; and later the Melchizedek Priesthood under the hands of former-day apostles, Peter, James, and John.[50]

Mormons claim the priesthoods of both Aaron and Melchizedek. They assert that John the Baptist conferred the Aaronic priesthood upon Joseph Smith and Oliver Cowdery on May 15, 1829. Shortly thereafter the priesthood of Melchizedek was conferred by Peter, James, and John. The Bible, quite to the contrary, teaches that the Aaronic (or

Levitical) priesthood was "changed" or done away, after the death of Christ. Hebrews 7:11-12 teaches:

> If therefore perfection were by the Levitical priesthood...what further need was there that another priest should rise after the order of Melchisedec, and not be called after the order of Aaron? For the priesthood being changed, there is made of necessity a change of the Law also.

When the law of God changed from the Old Testament to the New Testament, the priesthood of the descendants of Aaron became obsolete. Furthermore, the Bible specifies that the only ones who could occupy this priesthood in Old Testament times were descendants of Aaron. The Bible says in Exodus 29:9, "And thou shalt gird them with girdles, Aaron and his sons, and put bonnets on them: and the priest's office shall be their's for a perpetual statute: and thou shalt consecrate Aaron and his sons."

Other members of the tribe of Levi who did not descend from Aaron helped in them in their duties. In Numbers 3:6-7 the Bible says, "Bring the tribe of Levi near, and present them before Aaron the priest, that they may minister unto him. And they shall keep his charge, and the charge of the whole congregation before the tabernacle of the congregation, to do the service of the tabernacle."

Ironically, Mormons usually claim to be descendants of Ephraim or Manasseh, neither of whom was a descendent of Aaron. This, by their own admission, means they are not qualified to be priests.

The priesthood of Melchizedek was a unique position with only one occupant in the Old Testament. The Bible says:

> For this Melchisedec, king of Salem, priest of the most high God, who met Abraham returning from the slaughter of the kings, and blessed him; to whom also Abraham gave a tenth part of all; first being by interpretation King of righteousness, and after that also King of Salem, which is, king of peace; without father, without

mother, without descent, having neither beginning of days, nor end of life; but made like unto the Son of God; abideth a priest continually [Hebrews 7:1-3].

That unique office is now filled by the only other occupant, Jesus Christ. Hebrews 7:17 states, "Thou art a priest for ever after the order of Melchisedec."

There is no need for such priesthoods today because, first, Jesus Christ is our great high priest. The Bible says, "For there is one God, and one mediator between God and men, the man Christ Jesus" (1 Timothy 2:5). Second, every Christian is a spiritual priest serving under Christ. Peter wrote, "But ye are...a royal priesthood" (1 Peter 2:9). The existence of physical priests in the Christian era violates the Bible teaching of the priesthood of believers and implies that the continuing mediatorial work of Jesus Christ is insignificant. One author accurately summed up the Mormon priesthood and its relationship to the Biblical offices:

> Today the Mormon church claims a priesthood that includes deacons in their teens, and nonagenarian presidents. Boys hold the lesser, or Aaronic priesthood; elders are ordained to the Melchizedek priesthood at maturity and as they qualify. The names of the two priesthoods are the only element that lends a religious flavor to the structure of the priesthood. There is no similarity between the biblical rituals and priestly services of the Old Testament and the rituals of the Mormon church.[51]

Doctrine of Blood Atonement

Blood atonement is the Mormon doctrine that some sins are so grievous that only the shedding of the sinner's blood can atone for them. Brigham Young defined this tenet as follows:

> It is true that the blood of the Son of God was shed for sins through the fall and those committed by men, yet men can commit sins which it can never remit....There are sins that can be atoned for by an offering upon an altar, as in ancient days; and

there are sins that the blood of a lamb, of a calf, or of turtle doves, cannot remit, but they must be atoned for by the blood of the man.[52]

Young further said in *Journal of Discourses:*

Suppose you find your brother in bed with your wife, and put a javelin through both of them, you would be justified, and they would atone for their sins and be received into the kingdom of God.[53]

While Mormons do not, to our knowledge, practice this doctrine today, they still believe that some sins are beyond the atoning work of Jesus Christ. The Bible teaches, to the contrary, that if a Christian commits any sin, he must only repent of and confess it, and God will forgive him. In 1 John 1:9 we read, "If we confess our sins, he is faithful and just to forgive us our sins, and to cleanse us from all unrighteousness."

Miscellaneous False Prophecies

While the term "prophet" usually brings to mind foretelling the future, biblically a prophet was simply an inspired teacher. Isaiah was functioning as a prophet when he foretold the fall of Babylon before that great city even rose. He was also exercising his prophetic gift when reproving the people of God for their sins and exhorting them to holier living. God told the Israelites that to determine who was a true prophet and who was not, they must evaluate the accuracy of their predictions. Deuteronomy 18:20-22 states:

But the prophet, which shall presume to speak a word in my name, which I have not commanded him to speak, or shall speak in the name of other gods, even that prophet shall die. And if thou say in thine heart, How shall we know the word which the Lord hath not spoken? When a prophet speaketh in the name of the Lord, if the thing follow not, nor come to pass, that is the thing which the Lord hath not spoken, but the prophet hath spoken it presumptuously: thou shall not be afraid of him.

The test was quite simple. If a prophet predicts a future event which does not come to pass, he is not a true prophet and is to be disregarded. Observe that to be disregarded he needs to miss only one prophecy. A true prophet of God was one hundred percent accurate. Isaiah expressed that sentiment as he challenged the false prophets of his day. Isaiah 41:22-23 declares:

> Let them bring them forth, and shew us what shall happen: let them shew the former things, what they be, that we may consider them, and know the latter end of them; or declare us things for to come. Shew the things that are to come hereafter, that we may know that ye are gods: yea, do good, or do evil, that we may be dismayed, and behold it together.

Clearly, if Joseph Smith or any other Mormon "prophet" has ever uttered anything in the name of the Lord which did not come to pass, then he is a false prophet and is not to be feared.

Joseph Smith taught that the sun and moon were inhabited. He said, according to *Young Woman's Journal,* that there were moon dwellers who were six feet tall, dressing like Quakers and living 1,000 years.[54] Brigham Young, when later asked about this statement, concurred and said they were also living on the sun.[55] Modern science has, of course, shown this so-called "prophetic insight" to be pure nonsense. We needn't go any further; that single false prophesy, according to Deuteronomy 18, is enough to lead the sincere follower of God to disregard both of these men. There is, however, a wealth of false prophesies in Mormonism.

Smith predicted that the United States Government would be overthrown. He asserted that unless the U.S. government redressed the wrongs done to the Mormons by the state of Missouri, in only a few years the nation would be "utterly overthrown and wasted," and there would "not be so much as a potsherd left."[56] Almost one hundred and fifty years have passed since this prophecy, and the U. S. government hasn't redressed any wrongs done to the Latter-day Saints by the state of Missouri. The federal government has yet to be utterly wasted.

Smith prophesied great famine would come upon the United States. In not too many years from the time he spoke, Smith predicted, "Bloodshed..., pestilence, hail, famine, and earthquake will sweep the wicked of this generation from off the face of the land." He went on to say, "There are those now living upon the earth whose eyes shall not be closed in death until they see all these things, which I have spoken, fulfilled."

Smith claimed that these terrible events were to "prepare the way for the return of the lost tribes of Israel from the north country."[57] Again we have a prophecy about one hundred and fifty years old. Where has been the pestilence and famine described in this statement? Where is evidence that lost tribes have thus returned?

Smith predicted that the inhabitants of the earth in his generation would be visited with utter desolation. He said, "I prophesy, in the name of the Lord God of Israel, anguish and wrath and tribulation and the withdrawing of the Spirit of God from the earth await this generation, until they are visited with utter destruction."[58] Once again, one of Smith's gloom and doom predictions has failed to materialize.

Smith predicted the Civil War would involve all nations. Much has been said and written by the Mormon church concerning Joseph Smith's so-called prophecy of the civil war. Mormons believe it to be absolute proof of Smith's prophetic ability. The prophecy in its entirety is found in *Doctrine and Covenants*, section 87. For the purposes of this book verses 3 and 4 are considered:

> For behold, the Southern States shall be divided against the Northern States, and the Southern States will call on other nations, even the nation of Great Britain, as it is called, and they shall also call upon other nations, in order to defend themselves

against other nations; and then war shall be poured out upon all nations. And it shall come to pass, after many days, slaves shall rise up against their masters, who shall be marshaled and disciplined for war.

What Mormons overlook is that newspapers were full of articles of the possibility of the secession of South Carolina at the time of this supposed "oracle." While the civil war which had been expected and dreaded for many years did occur, Smith falsely predicted a world war, prophesying that all nations would participate. As even casual students of the era well know, there was no widespread rebellion of slaves. Joseph Smith was not exercising the gift of prophecy, but rather was reflecting the common concerns of his time.

Smith predicted that the Nauvoo house would belong to the Smith family forever. This "prophesy" is found in *Doctrine and Covenants* 124:56-60. Smith was killed in 1844. The Mormons were driven from Nauvoo, and the house has not since been the possession of the Smith family.

Smith predicted that Christ would come within fifty-six years. According to *History of the Church,* "Those who went to Zion, with a determination to lay down their lives, if necessary, should be ordained to the ministry, and go forth to prune the vineyard for the last time, or the coming of the Lord, which was nigh—even fifty-six years should wind up the scene."[59] That prophesy was made in 1835. The facts speak for themselves concerning its truthfulness.

Smith's father predicted that Joseph Smith, Jr. would continue in the priest's office until the second coming of Christ. Smith apparently considered this prophecy genuine since he later related:

Among the number, my father presented himself, but before I washed his feet, I asked of him a father's blessing, which he granted by laying his hands upon my head, in the name of Jesus Christ, and declaring that I should continue in the Priest's office until Christ comes.[60]

Smith was murdered in 1844 and Christ has yet to come.

Young taught that the blood of Jews changes when they become Mormons. He declared:

> If a Jew comes into this Church, and honestly professes to be a Saint, a follower of Christ, and if the blood of Judah is in his veins, he will apostatize. He may have been born and bred a Jew, have the face of a Jew, speak the language of the Jews, and have attended to all the ceremonies of the Jewish religion, and have openly professed to be a Jew all his days; but I will tell you a secret—there is not a particle of the blood of Judaism in him, if he has become a true Christian, a Saint of God; for if there is, he will most assuredly leave the Church of Christ.[61]

The Bible nowhere teaches that there are different types of blood that must be changed for proper obedience to God. Rather it declares that God "hath made of one blood all nations of men for to dwell on all the face of the earth" (Acts 17:26).

Young taught that minerals grow. Brigham Young, the man who taught, "I have never yet preached a sermon and sent it out to the children of men, that they may not call Scripture,"[62] said in a sermon, "Gold and silver grow, and so does every other kind of metal, the same as the hair on my head, or the wheat in the field."[63]

Young taught that killing apostates was a good work. He declared, "I say, rather than that apostates should flourish here I will unsheath my bowie knife, and conquer or die....Let us call upon the Lord to assist us in this, and in every good work."[64]

Clearly, freedom of religion was not highly treasured in Utah during Young's life. More importantly, this teaching shows Brigham to be the false prophet he was. Particularly noteworthy is the stark contrast of that tenet with the teaching of Christ. The Bible relates an incident at the time of Christ's arrest.

And, behold, one of them which were with Jesus stretched out his hand, and drew his sword, and struck a servant of the high priest's, and smote off his ear. Then said Jesus unto him, Put up again thy sword into his place: for all they that take the sword shall perish with the sword [Matthew 26:51-52].

Christ further declared, "My kingdom is not of this world; if my kingdom were of this world, then would my servants fight" (John 18:36). The kingdom of Joseph and Brigham may be defended by knife and gun, but not the kingdom of Christ. It is difficult to imagine a clearer example of the discord between the teachings of Mormonism and the Bible.

Young predicted that Mormon elders would be like kings. He prognosticated on August 26, 1856, "Twenty-six years will not pass away before the Elders of this Church will be as much thought of as the kings on their thrones."[65] Amazingly, almost twenty-six years later, on March 22, 1882, the Edmunds Act was passed against polygamy in Utah. Far from being treated as kings on thrones, the Mormons suffered what is probably their most humiliating defeat.

Young predicted slavery would not end. He declared, "Ham will continue to be the servant of servants, as the Lord has decreed, until the curse is removed. Will the present struggle free the slave? No."[66] The failure of that so-called prophecy is so obvious there is no need for comment.

Young declared that to get to heaven, one must have a passport from Joseph Smith. He said, "Every man and woman must have the certificate of Joseph Smith, Junior, as a passport to their entrance into the mansion where God and Christ are."[67] In reality the only passport to heaven is Jesus Christ. The Bible says in 1 John 14:2-3, "In my Father's house are many mansions: if it were not so, I would have told you. I go to prepare a place for you. And if I go and prepare a place for you, I will come again, and receive you unto myself; that where I am, there ye may be also."

Brigham Young predicted that Mormons would never deny the principle of polygamy. He said, "Do you think that we shall ever be admitted as a state into the Union without denying the principle of polygamy? If we are not admitted until then, we shall never be admitted."[68] The Latter-day Saints disavowed polygamy only a few decades after that statement was made.

Heber Kimball, one of the original Mormon apostles and First Counselor to Brigham Young, prophesied that Young would become President. He predicted, "The Church and kingdom to which we belong will become the kingdom of our God and his Christ, and brother Brigham Young will become president of the United States."[69] History has shown this prophesy, too, to be false.

Heber Kimball revealed that the earth conceives. He declared:

> Does the earth conceive? It does, and it brings forth. If it did not, why do you go and put your wheat in the ground? Does it not conceive it?...It conceives and brings forth, and you and I live, both for food and for clothing, silks and satins....Where did the earth come from?...From its parent earths.[70]

Conclusion

The false doctrines of Mormonism stand as proof positive that the LDS faith was begun by a false teacher—Joseph Smith, Jr.—and has been continued by false teachers. Deep love for all mankind has moved God to place in the Bible clear warnings against purveyors of religious error. The Word of God warns in I John 4:1, "Beloved, believe not every spirit, but try the spirits whether they are of God: because many false prophets are gone out into the world."

Again, 2 John 10-11 says, "If there come any unto you, and bring not this doctrine, receive him not into your house, neither bid him God speed: for he that biddeth him God speed is partaker of his evil deeds." Paul wrote, "If any man think himself to be a prophet, or spiritual, let him acknowledge that the things that I write unto you are the commandments of the Lord" (I Corinthians 14:37). In other words, had Smith actually been a spokesman for God he would have simply pointed to the Bible and said, "Therein lies the truth."

Notes

1. David Whitmer, *An Address to All Believers in Christ* (Richmond, Missouri: By the author, 1887), 35.

2. *Journal of Discourses*, Vol. 13, p. 264.

3. Brigham Young stated in *Journal of Discourses*, Vol. 3, p. 266, "Now if any of you will deny the plurality of wives and continue to do so, I promise that you will be damned; and I will go still further, and say take this revelation, or any other revelation that the Lord has given, and deny it in your feelings, and I promise that you will be damned."

4. Scott, *The Mormon Mirage*, 110.

5. Smith, *Doctrine and Covenants*, 132:52, 61-62.

6. Ibid., pp. 256-257.

7. *Journal of Discourses*, Vol. 1, pp. 50-51.

8. Whitmer, *An Address to All Believers in Christ*, 30-31.

9. W.E. Vine, *Expository Dictionary of New Testament Words* (Old Tappan, New Jersey: Fleming H. Revell Co., 1966), 173-174.

10. Smith, *Teachings of the Prophet Joseph Smith,* 349.

11. *Journal of Discourses*, Vol. 7, p. 333.

12. Bruce R. McConkie, *Mormon Doctrine* (Salt Lake City: Bookcraft, 1979), 516.

13. *Principles of the Gospel* (Church of Jesus Christ of Latter-day Saints, 1976), 184.

14. Parley P. Pratt, *Key to the Science of Theology* (Salt Lake City: Deseret Book Co., 1978), repr., 23.

15. Ibid., 18.

16. *Journal of Discourses*, Vol. 1, p. 123.

17. *Journal of Discourses*, Vol. 6, p. 126.

18. McConkie, *Mormon Doctrine*, 576-577.

19. Smith, *Doctrine and Covenants* 20:17, 19.

20. *Journal of Discourses*, Vol. 1, p. 50.

21. *Journal of Discourses*, Vol. 4, p. 218.

22. *Journal of Discourses*, Vol. 8, p. 115.

23. *Journal of Discourses*, Vol. 1, p. 50.

24. Orson Pratt, *Millennial Star*, Vol. 17, p. 195.

25. Bruce R. McConkie to Eugene England, 19 February 1981, Transcript in the hand of Utah Lighthouse Ministry, Salt Lake City.

26. *Journal of Discourses*, Vol. 13, p. 264.

27. Pratt, *Key to the Science of Theology*, 20.

28. *Journal of Discourses*, Vol. 2, pp. 81-82.

29. *Journal of Discourses*, Vol. 4, p. 210.

30. Smith, *Pearl*, Book of Moses 5:13

31. McConkie, *Mormon Doctrine*, 752.

32. Smith, *Doctrine and Covenants*, 130:22.

33. McConkie, *Mormon Doctrine*, 753.

34. Smith, *Teachings of the Prophet Joseph Smith*, 149.

35. Smith, *Doctrine and Covenants*, 93:29, 33.

36. *Journal of Discourses*, Vol. 1, p. 50.

37. Bruce McConkie, *Mormon Doctrine*, 1966 ed., pp. 108-109, quoted in Walter Martin, *The Maze of Mormonism* (Ventura: Regal Books, 1962), 179.

38. *Journal of Discourses*, Vol. 7, p. 290.

39. *Journal of Discourses*, Vol. 10, p. 110.

40. Joseph Fielding Smith, *Doctrines of Salvation*, Vol. 1, p. 114.

41. Smith, *Teachings of the Prophet Joseph Smith*, 346-347.

42. Lorenzo Snow, *Improvement Era*, June 1919, 660, quoted in Daniel H. Ludlow, *Latter-Day Prophets Speak* (Daniel H. Ludlow, 1948), 71-72.

43. James E. Talmage, *A Study of the Articles of Faith*, Missionary Reference Set Ed. (Salt Lake City: Deseret Book Co., 1983), 214.

44. Ibid., 215.

45. Smith, *Teachings of the Prophet Joseph Smith*, 327.

46. *Journal of Discourses*, Vol. 11, pp. 125-126.

47. Talmage, *Articles of Faith*, 16.

48. Smith, *Doctrine and Covenants*, 127:6.

49. McConkie, *Mormon Doctrine*, 308-309.

50. Talmage, *Articles of Faith*, 185.

51. Fraser, *Is Mormonism Christian?*, 87.

52. *Journal of Discourses*, Vol. 4, p. 54.

53. *Journal of Discourses*, Vol. 3, p. 247.

54. Oliver B. Huntington, "Inhabitants of the Moon," *Young Woman's Journal*, 3 (1892), 263.

55. *Journal of Discourses*, Vol. 13, p. 271.

56. Smith, *History of the Church*, Vol. V, p. 394.

57. Smith, *History of the Church*, Vol. I, pp. 315-316.

58. Smith, *History of the Church*, Vol. VI, p. 58.

59. Smith, *History of the Church*, Vol. II, p. 182.

60. Smith, *History of the Church*, Vol. I, p. 323.

61. *Journal of Discourses*, Vol. 2, p. 142.

62. *Journal of Discourses*, Vol. 13, p. 95.

63. *Journal of Discourses*, Vol. 1, p. 219.

64. Ibid., 83.

65. *Journal of Discourses*, Vol. 4, p. 40.

66. *Journal of Discourses*, Vol. 10, p. 250.

67. *Journal of Discourses*, Vol. 7, p. 289.

68. *Journal of Discourses*, Vol. 11, p. 269.

69. *Journal of Discourses*, Vol. 5, p. 219.

70. *Journal of Discourses*, Vol. 6, p. 36.

Chapter 5

Can the Bible Be Trusted?

Those with beliefs which obviously conflict with the Bible usually end up dealing with their differences with God's word by discrediting it. This is clearly illustrated in the case of Mormonism. LDS leader James E. Talmage declared that Latter-day Saints accept the Bible as "the Word of God as far as it is correctly translated." Mormon authorities present to their people a picture of copies of copies being made until today's Bible is far from what was originally penned by inspired writers in the first century. The *Book of Mormon* set the tone for that attitude toward the Bible.

Referring to the fact that the Bible was accurate when it first "went forth," Nephi declared:

> Wherefore, these things go forth from the Jews in purity unto the Gentiles....And after they go forth..., thou seest the formation of that great and abominable church [the Roman Catholic Church], which is most abominable above all other churches; for behold, they have taken away from the gospel of the Lamb many parts which are plain and most precious; and also many covenants of the Lord have they taken away...that they may pervert the right

ways of the Lord, that they might blind the eyes and harden the hearts of the children of men....because of the many plain and precious things which have been taken out of the book [the Bible],...an exceedingly great many do stumble, yea, insomuch that Satan hath great power over them [I Nephi 13:25-27, 29].

Mormon theologian James E. Talmage wrote in *Articles of Faith:*

There will be, there can be, no absolutely reliable translation of these or other scriptures unless it is effected through the gift of translation, as one of the endowments of the Holy Ghost....Let the Bible then be read reverently and with prayerful care, the reader ever seeking the light of the Spirit that he may discern between truth and the errors of men.[1]

Similarly, Orson Pratt asked, "Who knows that even one verse of the whole Bible has escaped pollution, so as to convey the same sense now that it did in the original?"[2] Clearly, LDS religion is cradled in the rejection of the reliability of the Bible.

Contempt for the Word of God is seen in the early history of Mormonism. From the time the angel Moroni supposedly appeared to Joseph Smith, quoting passages differently from the way they are found in the Bible, the faith of Latter-day Saints has been characterized by a lack of respect for the Bible. This is no more clearly illustrated than in the existence of the so-called *Inspired Version*, the supposedly corrected version of the Bible which Joseph Smith produced.

Examining the *Inspired Version* we find, not a translation correction at all, but sweeping changes in the text of the Bible, particularly in Genesis and Matthew chapter 24. In Genesis 1:6, God speaks in the first person: "And I, God, said, Let there be light." In Genesis chapter 2:6-9 the Mormon doctrine of the preexistence of the souls of men has been inserted.

And I, the Lord God, had created all the children of men, and not yet a man to till the ground, for in heaven I created them, and there was not yet flesh upon the earth, neither in the water, neither in the air; Nevertheless, all things were before created, but spiritually they were created and made.[3]

Genesis 3:1-5 records Satan coming before God and asking to be savior of the world. When God refused, the devil rebelled. In Genesis 6:67, the *Inspired Version* has the alleged account of Adam's baptism by immersion, administered miraculously by the Spirit of the Lord. A section is added giving the prophecy of Enoch, saying that not only Enoch, but also an entire group of saints, the people of Zion, were taken up into heaven (Genesis 6:26—7:78).

Smith's most brazen alteration of the Bible is found in Genesis 50:33, a thirty-four word verse, which is "corrected" to over 800 words. In this passage, the last words of Joseph, son of Israel, are expanded to include a prediction of Moses. "The Prophet's" boldness in amending God's will reaches its zenith with Joseph Smith, Jr. including a prediction of himself:

> And that seer will I bless, and they that seek to destroy him shall be confounded; for this promise I give unto you; for I will remember you from generation to generation; and his name shall be called Joseph, and it shall be after his father; and he shall be like unto you; for the thing which the Lord shall bring forth by his hand shall bring my people unto salvation.[4]

The Reorganized Church, the group headquartered in Independence, Missouri, continues to publish and use this version. While some Utah adherents use it, the main body of Mormons neither prints nor officially recognizes the *Inspired Version*. The reason given is that Smith was killed before he could finish his work of revision. Referring to the King James Version, Brigham Young said:

> That made us very anxious in the days of Joseph, to get the new translation; but the Bible is good enough just as it is, it will answer my purpose, and it was used to answer it very well when I was preaching in the world.[5]

The reluctance of the Utah Mormons to use Smith's version raises several questions. Completed or not, Joseph Smith had a revelation that the *Inspired Version* was to be published. In *Doctrine and Covenants* 94:10 we read:

> Verily I say unto you, the second lot on the south shall be dedicated unto me for the building of a house unto me, for the work of the printing of the translation of my scriptures, and all things whatsoever I shall command you.

The failure of the Utah church to publish this version is tantamount to disobedience to *Doctrine and Covenants*, and therefore amounts to a rejection of Smith's authority as a prophet.

Even if it is granted that the work of correcting the Scriptures was not completed by Smith, would it not be sensible to publish the *Inspired Version* and benefit from as many corrections as were made? Surely it is better to have a Bible with some errors corrected than one with no corrections at all. It appears that the church headquartered in Salt Lake City is more than a little embarrassed by the version. Perhaps leaders there suspect that it is not a translation correction at all but a blatant rewriting of substantial parts of the Bible.

But how about the "uncorrected" Bible? Not Joseph Smith's version, but the real thing—can it be trusted? The answer is a resounding "Yes!"

Manuscript Evidence Shows the Bible Is Trustworthy

We do not have the original manuscripts of the Old or New Testament books. In other words, the first document of the book of Matthew is not in existence, as far as can be determined, nor does the original Revelation manuscript actually penned by John exist. Undoubtedly the "autographs," as they are called, were circulated among churches and read until they became tattered, then discarded.

Some are surprised to learn this, since the autographs of many famous books are in existence. For example, the autobiography of Benjamin Franklin in his own handwriting, as well as the original manuscript of a Jack London novel, have been displayed in recent years in a library in the Los Angeles area. When the manuscript evidence of the New Testament is examined, however, it must be compared, not with the literature of our times, but with other ancient writings.

For Caesar's *Gallic War* (composed between 58 and 50 B.C.) there are only nine or ten good manuscripts, the oldest being about 900 years after Caesar's time. The most recent copy was made almost 1,000 years after Caesar's death. In spite of the long interval between the date of writing and available copies of that work, scholars all accept the manuscripts as accurately relating Caesar's original work.

Of the 142 books of the *Roman History of Livy* (59 B.C.—A.D. 17), only thirty-five survive; these are known to us from less than twenty manuscripts, only one of which is as old as the fourth century. In other words, the most recent manuscript was copied almost five hundred years after Livy completed his work. Today's text of the *History of Livy* is considered an accurate record of what was originally written.

The same is true of the *History of Herodotus* (480-425 B.C.). The earliest copy of the eight ancient manuscripts still in existence is from A.D. 900, almost 1300 years after the actual time of authorship. Those manuscripts are universally accepted as accurately reflecting the work of the great Herodotus.[6]

Homer was the most widely read author of antiquity. In 900 B.C. he wrote *Illiad*. The earliest copy of *Illiad* is from 400 B.C., 500 years after the time of authorship. There are 643 ancient copies of *Illiad* in existence, and its current text is considered reliable.[7]

The New Testament was written between A.D. 40 and 100. The earliest copy of a New Testament document is a fragment from A.D. 125, only 25 years from the date of the actual writing. There are over 24,000 ancient manuscripts of New Testament writings; 5300 are in the Greek language in which it was originally written. In addition to that over-whelming amount of evidence, 32,000 citations of New Testament passages are found in uninspired writings penned before A.D. 325. The New Testament can virtually be reconstructed by these citations alone.

With all of this manuscript evidence, only $\frac{1}{1000}$ of the text is subject to variation, and none of the variations involves an issue of faith. Textual critic F.F. Bruce observed, "The variant readings about which any doubt remains among textual critics of the New Testament affects no material question of historic fact or of Christian faith and practice."[8]

To summarize, there is a teacup of evidence that Caesar actually wrote what he is believed to have written, but it is universally accepted. There is a pail of evidence that Homer actually wrote the works attributed to him, yet it is accepted by all. Comparatively speaking, there is an Olympic sized swimming pool of evidence that the New Testament, as originally written, is what we have today. Confirmation of the present New Testament text is absolutely overwhelming.

The oldest manuscripts of the Old Testament are the Dead Sea Scrolls, from as early as 100 B.C. Excluding those, the earliest Hebrew manuscripts are from A.D. 895. We come to deeply respect the integrity of the present Old Testament text when the methods of the early copyists are considered. Their approach has been described as one of "superstitious perfectionism."

The Talmudists made copies of the Old Testament from A.D. 100 to 500. The following minute regulations guided the work of these scribes: Copies must be written on skins of clean animals, fastened together with strings from clean animals, prepared by a Jew. Every skin must contain a certain number of columns. The length of each column must be between forty-eight and sixty lines, and the breadth of each line must consist of thirty letters. The copy must first be lined and if three words are written without a line, it is worthless. The ink must be black, prepared according to a certain recipe. The copy must be made from an accurate manuscript and no word is to be copied from memory. Between every consonant must be a space of a hair or thread. Between each section must be a space of nine consonants. There must be three lines between each book. The fifth book of Moses must terminate exactly with a line. The copyist must sit in full Jewish dress, wash his body, and not begin to write the name of God with a pen newly dipped in ink.[9]

From A.D. 500 to 900, the Massoretes reproduced Old Testament Scriptures. These scribes sought a method to totally eliminate scribal errors and nearly achieved it by developing an intricate system of counting. They counted the number of times each letter appeared in each book, and calculated the middle letter of both the Pentateuch and the entire Old Testament. The verses, words, and letters of each book were counted. All the verses which contained all the letters of the alphabet were noted. The middle verse, middle word, and middle letter of each book was determined and checked with each copy. The Massoretes counted the number of letters in each book.

It has been said of their work, "Everything that could have been counted seems to have been." Upon completion a manuscript had to check out flawlessly through these counting procedures or it was discarded. The result of such rigorous guidelines is that in comparing manuscripts from the ninth and tenth centuries with the Dead Sea Scrolls produced a thousand years before, there is no significant difference.

King James of England began a tradition of translating the Bible into English using a large group of translators. In 1607, forty-eight scholars formally began the translation of the version. They were divided into six working companies, two at Oxford, two at Cambridge, and two at Westminster. Each company, guided by detailed instructions, was assigned books of the Bible to be translated. The translations then had to be reviewed and approved by the other companies, and delegates from each company were assigned to resolve differences. Clearly, the King James Version was truly translated by all forty-eight scholars.

The conclusion is obvious: the Bible is reliable and trustworthy. Isaiah, by the power of inspiration, expressed it thus: "The grass withereth, the flower fadeth; but the word of our God shall stand forever" (Isaiah 40:8).

Archaeology Confirms that the Bible Is Trustworthy

Archaeologist John Free stated, "The Bible is a historical book." As the field of archaeology is plumbed for evidence supporting the Bible record, confirmation of the accuracy of the Word of God repeatedly surfaces. Waves of critics have unleashed attacks of skepticism upon the historicity of the Bible, only to be repeatedly embarrassed as the excavator's spade revealed yet more evidence of its accuracy. Free continued:

> Certain critics have said that the accounts of Abraham are legendary, that Mosaic legislation was formulated hundreds of years after the time of Moses, that such people as the Hittites were either legendary or insignificant, that the book of Judges was composed of "good stories," and not really historical accounts, that various people ranging from Sargon to Sanballat were unhistorical. Yet archaeological discoveries have shown that these critical charges and countless others are wrong and that the Bible is trustworthy in the very statements which have been set aside as untrustworthy.[10]

Archaeology has been so supportive of the Bible text that it has shed light on previously confusing teachings in the Word of God. A passage that bewildered scholars was Deuteronomy 14:21 which directed Israelites, "Thou shalt not seethe a kid in his mother's milk." For centuries commentators gave confused and conflicting interpretations of that command. Archaeology uncovered the key to understanding the mystery with the discovery of the Ras Shamra tablets. Recording a similar rite, they indicate, "If one wishes to gain favor with a deity, he should slay a kid in milk."[11] In Deuteronomy 14 God was simply forewarning Israel of a pagan ritual she would be tempted to practice in the land of Canaan.

Critics have tried to date the writings the Bible which are attributed to Moses to a period much later than his lifetime. Repeatedly, however, archaeological evidence has shown them to be contemporary with Moses. For example, some have asserted that the account of Abraham in Genesis was recorded as late as 800 B.C. However, nearly all the towns connected with Abraham in the Bible have been excavated and have been proven to have flourished during Abraham's time. A later writer or Genesis would likely tell of cities which existed in his time but which did not exist in the patriarchal age.[12]

The pinpoint accuracy of the Word of God is seen in the account of the fall of Jericho. Jericho was excavated between 1929 and 1936. Dr. John Garstang, the excavator, surprised the archaeological community with the discovery that the walls of the city had fallen outward.[13] That came as no surprise to Bible-believing people, however, because Joshua 6:20 says:

> So the people shouted when the priests blew with the trumpets: and it came to pass, when the people heard the sound of the trumpet, and the people shouted with a great shout, that the wall fell down flat, so that the people went up into the city, every man straight before him, and they took the city.

It was also discovered that Jericho had been burned, along with a large quantity of grain stored within its walls. That is unusual for three reasons.

First, a siege (a military tactic in which the hostile armies surrounded a city allowing nothing to enter or leave) was the strategy almost always employed against a walled city. Its purpose was to starve the city into submission. Had defeat come after months or years under siege, the grain would have been eaten. The discovery of the charred grain, however, indicates that Jericho fell quickly. That is exactly in accord with the Bible account of Jericho's being destroyed in seven days (Joshua 6:15, 20).

Second, the presence of a great deal of grain indicates that the city fell near the end of or shortly after harvest. That harmonizes with the Bible which says that Rahab was drying flax on her roof (Joshua 2:6). And the Jordan River was flooded, something that occurred at harvest time (Joshua 3:15). Sieges, on the other hand, were typically carried out just before harvest when grain stores were low.[14] Third, the discovery of the grain is unusual since it was used as a medium of commerce at the time. Ordinarily, that and all other valuables would have been plundered by the conquering army.

The unprecedented tactic of putting the city to the torch harmonizes with the Bible, which reveals that "they burnt the city with fire, and all that was therein" (Joshua 6:24). God had specifically instructed them that the commodities in the city were not to be taken. Joshua commanded the people to keep themselves from "the accursed thing" (v. 18).[15]

Luke, the author of the book bearing his name as well as Acts, was accused of inaccuracy before the flourishing of archaeology. He was criticized for Luke 2:1-3, which says, "And it came to pass in those days, that there went out a decree from Caesar Augustus, that all the world should be taxed. (And this taxing was first made when Cyrenius

[Quirinius] was governor of Syria.) And all went to be taxed every one into his own city."

Critics said there was no census taken by Rome, that Quirinius was not governor of Syria at that time but later, and that everyone did not have to return to his ancestral home. Archaeological discoveries have clearly revealed, however, that the Romans had a regular enrollment of taxpayers and conducted a census every 14 years. The one to which Luke refers was probably the first census. Quirinius was governor at that time as well as later, and it is now clear that people did have to return to their homeland. The criticisms of that passage have been totally silenced.[16]

It was also assumed that Luke erred in Acts 17:6 when he wrote, "They drew Jason and certain brethren unto the rulers of the city." The term for those rulers is *politarchs*. It was surmised that since that word did not appear in classical literature, Luke was wrong and the office did not exist. Since then, nineteen inscriptions have been found which mention the title. Five of these inscriptions are in reference to Thessalonica, where the incident recorded in Acts 17:6 occurred.[17] Sir William Ramsay, one of the greatest archaeologists of all time, wrote, "Luke is a historian of the first rank. This author should be placed along with the very greatest of historians."[18]

On and on we could go. Archaeologist Werner Keller commented:

> In view of the overwhelming mass of authentic and well-attested evidence now available, as I thought of the skepticism criticism which from the eighteenth century onwards would fain have demolished the Bible altogether, there kept hammering on my brain this one sentence: "The Bible is right after all."[19]

Yale archaeologist Millar Burrows wrote, "On the whole...archaeological work has unquestionably strengthened confidence in the reliability of the Scriptural record.

More than one archaeologist has found his respect for the
Bible increased by the experience of excavation in Palestine."[20]

Nelson Glueck, a prominent Jewish archaeologist said,
"It may be stated categorically that no archaeological discovery has ever controverted a Biblical reference."[21] Archaeologist G. Ernest Wright, commenting on the notion that the
Bible is little more than mythology, stated, "Archaeology has
substantiated and illuminated the biblical story at so many
crucial points that no one can take seriously this position."[22]
There is a tremendous contrast between the powerful vote of
confidence given to the Bible by these eminent scientists and
the Smithsonian Institution's position on the *Book of Mormon*: "Smithsonian archaeologists see no direct connection
between the archaeology of the New World and the subject
matter of the book."[23]

Scientific Foreknowledge in the Bible
Demonstrates Its Trustworthiness

The Bible is not a science textbook, but at times it incidentally deals with science. In such instances it is always
accurate, thus indicating its divine origin. In fact, the Word
of God revealed several scientific truths thousands of years
before men discovered them.

After a lifetime of study, Herbert Spencer, the famous
nineteenth-century British philosopher, identified the five
basics of science: time, force, action, space and matter. Yet
that truth had been revealed thousands years before in Genesis 1:1, where the Bible says, "In the beginning [time] God
[force] created [action] the heaven [space] and the earth
[matter]."

Job 26:7 says of God, "He stretcheth out the north over
the empty place, and hangeth the earth upon nothing." People in Job's day viewed the matter differently. Some ancients
believed that the planet rested on the backs of four elephants

who stood on the back of a giant turtle. Others believed that the Greek mythological giant, Atlas, supported the earth on his shoulders. As we see from the passage in Job, however, the Bible eclipsed the mythology and common misconceptions of the time. Isaiah 40:22, in speaking of God, declares, "It is he that sitteth upon the circle of the earth." The Hebrew word for "circle" literally suggests a sphere. A common view in the time of Isaiah was that the earth was flat. Again, a scientific fact buried in the Bible attests to its divine origin.

Nineteenth-century mariner Matthew Fontaine Maury was for a while in his life confined to bed. His son, while reading the Bible to him during this illness, read Psalm 8:8, which mentions "the paths of the sea." Maury decided that if the Bible says there are paths in the sea, that must be the case. He went on to discover major shipping lanes and to revolutionize oceanography; later he became the founder of Annapolis Naval Academy.

The Bible teaches that the earth is wearing out in Psalm 102:26, Isaiah 51:6, and Hebrews 1:11. This is in harmony with the Second Law of Thermodynamics, which states that everything is running down. That law, discovered only recently by scientists, was common knowledge to careful students of God's word thousands of years ago.

Moses commanded that animals which died of themselves were not to be eaten. Leviticus 17:15 declares, "And every soul that eateth that which died of itself, or that which was torn with beasts, whether it be one of your own country, or a stranger, he shall both wash his clothes, and bathe himself in water, and be unclean until the even: then shall he be clean."

The health hazards posed by eating an animal which is found dead are now widely recognized. Clearly, Moses understood the danger of using a dead animal for food long before science did. Further, Genesis 1 states that living things reproduce "after their kind." While that verity may seem obvious, only a few hundred years ago it was believed that maggots and flies spontaneously generated from rotten meat.[24]

Obviously, the scientific knowledge evidenced in the Bible was very much ahead of its time. The reason is obvious—the author of the Bible is the author of true science. What a contrast is seen between the Word of God with its sublime revelation of even scientific truth and the *Book of Mormon* with its anachronistic references to compasses before they were invented and steel before it was developed.

The All-Sufficiency of the Bible Reveals Its Trustworthiness

There is no need for the prophet Joseph Smith or additional so-called inspired writings. God has always intended that the Bible provide everything necessary in the spiritual realm. In 2 Timothy 3:16-17 we read, "All scripture is given by inspiration of God, and is profitable for doctrine, for reproof, for correction, for instruction in righteousness: that the man of God may be perfect, thoroughly furnished unto all good works."

Think about the broad scope of functions of the Word of God described in those verses. The Bible supplies all required doctrine, reproves and corrects us, and even instructs us in righteousness. What other needs could man have? If the *Book of Mormon* were genuine, just what gaps in divine truth would it fill? Of course, there are no voids to be filled. God who knows all has provided man with a complete guide. No wonder the passage concludes by saying that the Bible "thoroughly furnishes" man "unto all good works."

James 1:25 reinforces the truth of the completeness of the Bible, stating, "But whoso looketh into the perfect law of liberty, and continueth therein, he being not a forgetful hearer, but a doer of the work, this man shall be blessed in his deed." The New Testament is described as "perfect," and with perfection there is no room for improvement. Solomon wrote, "I know that, whatever God doeth, it shall be for ever; nothing can be put to it, nor any thing taken from it; and God doeth it, that men should fear before him" (Ecclesiastes 3:14). Since God produced the Bible, it cannot be bettered by additions or subtractions.

The Word of God, completed in the first century, is all the revelation that sincere people need to properly do God's will. Christians are commanded to study it diligently. In 2 Timothy 2:15, God commands, "Study to shew thyself approved unto God, a workman that needeth not to be ashamed, rightly dividing the word of truth." As the Scripture points out, it must be "rightly divided," that is, accurately interpreted. Paul wrote to the church in ancient Thessalonica:

> For this cause also thank we God without ceasing, because, when ye received the Word of God which ye heard of us, ye received it not as the word of men, but as it is in the truth, the Word of God, which effectually worketh also in you that believe [1 Thessalonians 2:13].

The Scriptures provided all required truth then and they provide all required truth now. Spiritual growth comes, not from the latter day "oracles" of Joseph Smith and his followers, but from constant nourishment from the same revelation that guided Christians who worshiped under the oversight of Jesus' apostles. Peter admonished, "As newborn babes, desire the sincere milk of the word, that ye may grow thereby (1 Peter 2:2). When the truth is genuinely sought, the words of Christ will live in the heart. In Colossians 3:16 the Bible says, "Let the word of Christ dwell in you richly in all wisdom." Additional inspired books, if they did exist, would not be needed.

Long before the *Book of Mormon* was supposedly revealed in America, the apostle Paul declared in Romans 1:16, "For I am not ashamed of the gospel of Christ: for it is the power of God unto salvation to every one that believeth; to the Jew first and also to the Greek." He had complete power for salvation before Joseph Smith's "revelations" ever entered the picture. The events now found in the New Testament were recorded so that every good-hearted person can develop saving faith. John wrote:

> And many other signs truly did Jesus in the presence of his disciples, which are not written in this book: But these are written, that ye might believe that Jesus is the Christ, the Son of God; and that believing ye might have life through his name [John 20:30-31].

Jesus indicated the awesome importance of his words when he revealed that they will do more than produce faith. The divine utterances of the New Testament will judge all men eternally. Christ said in John 12:48, "He that rejecteth me, and receiveth not my words, hath one that judgeth him: the word that I have spoken, the same shall judge him in the last day." The words of Christ, not the *Book of Mormon, Doctrine and Covenants* or *Pearl of Great Price*, will serve as the standard for evaluating our lives on judgment day. Clearly, the only safe course is to be guided by the Bible and the Bible alone.

Inspired words earnestly caution that one of the most grievous sins possible is to add to the Word of God. Like watchdogs, Scriptures stand at the beginning, middle, and end of the Bible forbidding man-made additions to inspiration. At the beginning of the Bible, Deuteronomy 4:2 guards the sacred text with this stern warning: "Ye shall not add unto the word which I command you, neither shall ye diminish ought from it, that ye may keep the commandments of the Lord your God which I command you." In the middle of the Bible, Proverbs 30:6 declares, "Add thou not unto his words, lest he reprove thee, and thou be found a liar." At the end of the Bible, referring in context to the Book of Revelation and in principle to the whole Bible we read the following:

> For I testify unto every man that heareth the words of the prophecy of this book, If any man shall add unto these things, God shall add unto him the plagues that are written in this book: and if any man shall take away from the words of the book of this prophecy, God shall take away his part out of the book of life, and out of the holy city, and from the things which are written in this book [Revelation 22:18-19].

Rather than seek out new "scriptures," let us rejoice in the completeness and fullness of the Bible. Let us share the attitude of the Psalmist who wrote, "The law of the Lord is perfect, converting the soul; the testimony of the Lord is sure, making wise the simple" (Psalm 19:7). May the truth of Psalm 119:105 always be realized: "Thy word is a lamp unto my feet, and a light unto my path."

Notes

1.Talmage, *Articles of Faith*, 215.

2. Parker Pratt Robinson, *Orson Pratt's Works* (Salt Lake City:Publishers Press, 1959), 196.

3. Joseph Smith, Jr., *The Holy Scriptures Containing the Old and New Testaments, an Inspired Version of the Authorized Version* (Independence: Herald House Publishing, 1944), 13.

4. Joseph Smith, Jr., *Inspired Version*, 92.

5. *Journal of Discourses,* Vol. 3, p. 116.

6. F.F. Bruce, *The New Testament Documents* (Grand Rapids: Wm. B. Eerdmans Publishing Co., 1968), 16-17.

7. Norman L. Geisler and William E. Nix, *A General Introduction to the Bible* (Chicago: Moody Press, 1968), 43.

8. Bruce, *The New Testament Documents*, 19-20.

9. Samuel Davidson, *Hebrew Text of the Old Testament*, second ed. (London: Samuel Bagster & Sons, 1859), 89, quoted in Neil Lightfoot, *How We Got the Bible* (Austin: Sweet Publishing Company, 1961), 78-79.

10. Joseph P. Free, *Archaeology and Bible History* (Wheaton, Illinois: Scripture Press Publications, Inc., 1969), 1-2.

11. Ibid., 123.

12. Ibid., 53.

13. Bryant G. Wood, "Did the Israelites Conquer Jericho? A New Look at the Archaeological Evidence," *Biblical Archaeological Review*, XVI, 2 (March/April 1990), 49.

14. Ibid., 51.

15. Ibid., 57.

16. F.F. Bruce, *The New Testament Documents* (Grand Rapids: Wm. B. Eerdmans Publishing Co., 1968), 86-87.

17. F.F. Bruce, "Archaeological Confirmation of the New Testament," chap. in *Revelation and the Bible: Contemporary Evangelical Thought,* ed. Carl Henry (Grand Rapids: Baker Book House, 1958), 325.

18. W.M. Ramsay, *The Bearing of Recent Discovery on the Trustworthiness of the New Testament* (London: Hodder and Stoughton, 1915), 222.

19. Werner Keller, *The Bible as History* (New York: William Morrow & Co., 1981), 24.

20. Millar Burrows, *What Mean These Stones?* (New York: Meridian Books, 1956), 1.

21. Nelson Glueck, *Rivers in the Desert: A History of the Negev* (New York: Farrar, Straus & Cudahy, 1959), 31.

22. G. Ernest Wright, *Biblical Archaeology* (Philadelphia: The Westminster Press, 1960), x.

23. The Smithsonian Institution, *Statement Regarding the Book of Mormon*, 1.

24. Bert Thompson, *Scientific Evidences of the Bible's Inspiration* (Montgomery, Alabama: Apologetics Press, 1981), used by permission.

Bibliography

Apostasy and Restoration. Salt Lake City: Corporation of the President of the Church of Jesus Christ of Latter-day Saints, 1983.

Brigham Young University Travel Study Update. Provo, Utah: Brigham Young University, Winter, 1990.

Brodie, Fawn McKay. *No Man Knows My History*. New York: Alfred A. Knopf, 1946.

Bruce, F.F. "Archaeological Confirmation of the New Testament." In *Revelation and the Bible*, ed. Carl Henry. Grand Rapids: Baker Book House, 1969, pp. 319-331.

_____. *The New Testament Documents*. Grand Rapids: Wm. B. Eerdmans Publishing Co., 1968.

Burrows, Millar. *What Mean These Stones?* New York: Meridian Books, 1956.

Campbell, Alexander. "Delusions." *Millennial Harbinger*, Vol. II, February 1831, 85-100.

Cowan, Marvin. *Mormon Claims Answered*. By the author: n.p., 1975.

Department of Anthropology, The Smithsonian Institution. *Statement Regarding the Book of Mormon*. Washington: National Museum of Natural History, Spring, 1986.

Daily Universe. Brigham Young University, Dec. 1, 1967. Quoted in Jerald and Sandra Tanner. *Mormonism-Shadow or Reality?* Salt Lake City: Modern Microfilm Co., 1972.

Free, Joseph P. *Archaeology and Bible History*. Wheaton, Illinois: Scripture Press Publications, Inc., 1969.

Geisler, Norman L. and William E. Nix. *A General Introduction to the Bible*. Chicago: Moody Press, 1968.

Glueck, Nelson. *Rivers in the Desert: History of Negev*. Philadelphia: Jewish Publications Society of America, 1969.

Hinckley, Gordon, *Truth Restored*. Salt Lake City: Corporation of the President, The Church of Jesus Christ of Latter-day Saints, 1979.

_____. *Truth Restored: Gospel Principles.* n.p.: Corporation of the President, The Church of Jesus Christ of Latter-day Saints, 1988.

Historical Magazine, News Series, Vol. 8, No. 5, November, 1870, pp. 315-316. Quoted in Walter Martin. *Kingdom of the Cults.* Minneapolis: Bethany House Publishers, 1985.

Hoekema, Anthony A. *Mormonism.* Grand Rapids: William B. Eerdmans Publishing Co., 1974.

Howe, E.D. *Mormonism Unvailed, or a faithful account of that singular imposition and delusion, from its rise to the present time.* Painesville, Ohio: By the author, 1834.

Huntington, Oliver B. "The Inhabitants of the Moon." *Young Woman's Journal,* Vol. 3, pp. 263-264.

Journal of Discourses. Twenty-six vols. Liverpool: F.D. Richards, Latter-day Saints' Book Depot, 1854-1886.

Keller, Werner. *The Bible as History.* New York: William Morrow & Co., 1981.

Kenyon, Frederic. *Our Bible and the Ancient Manuscripts.* Revised by A.W. Adams. New York: Harper and Brothers, 1958.

Kelly, Charles and Hoffman Birney. *Holy Murder: The Story of Porter Rockwell.* New York: Minton, Balch & Company, 1934.

Lamb, M.T. *The Golden Bible, or, The Book of Mormon, Is It From God?* New York: Ward & Drummond, 1887.

Lee, John D. *Mormonism Unveiled; or the Life and Confessions of John D. Lee.* St. Louis: Bryan, Brand & Company, 1877.

Linn, William Alexander. *The Story of the Mormons From the Date of Origin to the Year 1901.* London: Macmillan Company, 1902.

McConkie, Bruce R. *Mormon Doctrine.* Salt Lake City: Bookcraft, 1979.

_____. *Mormon Doctrine.* Salt Lake City: Bookcraft, 1966. Quoted in Walter Martin. *The Maze of Mormonism.* Ventura: Regal Books, 1985.

McConkie, Bruce R. to Eugene England, 19 February 1981, Transcript in the hand of Utah Lighthouse Ministry, Salt Lake City.

Nibley, Hugh. *An Approach to the Book of Mormon.* Salt Lake City: Deseret News Press, 1964.

Pratt, Orson. *Millennial Star,* Vol. 17, 1855.

Pratt, Parley P. *Key to the Science of Theology.* Salt Lake City: Deseret Book Co., 1978, reprint.

Principles of the Gospel. n.p.: Church of Jesus Christ of Latter-day Saints, 1976.

Ralston, Russell F. *Fundamental Differences Between the Reorganized Church and the Utah Church.* Independence, Missouri: Herald Publishing House, 1963.

Ramsey, W.M. *The Bearing of Recent Discovery on the Trustworthiness of the New Testament.* London: Hodder and Stoughton, 1920.

Robinson, Parker Pratt. *Orson Pratt's Works.* Salt Lake City: Publishers Press, 1959.

Scott, Latayne Colvett. *The Mormon Mirage.* Grand Rapids: Zondervan Publishing House, 1979.

Smith, Joseph Jr. *Book of Mormon.* Palmyra, New York: Egbert E. Grandin, 1830.

_____. *Book of Mormon.* Salt Lake City: Corporation of the President of the Church of Jesus Christ of Latter-day Saints, 1981.

_____. *Doctrine and Covenants.* Salt Lake City: The Church of Jesus Christ of Latter-day Saints, 1974.

_____. *The History of the Church of Jesus Christ of Latter-day Saints.* Six vols. Salt Lake City: Deseret News, 1902-1912.

_____. *The Holy Scriptures Containing the Old and New Testaments, an Inspired Version of the Authorized Version.* Independence: Herald House Publishing, 1944.

_____. *Pearl of Great Price.* Salt Lake City: The Church of Jesus Christ of Latter-day Saints, 1974.

Smith, Joseph Fielding, compiler. *Teachings of the Prophet Joseph Smith.* Salt Lake City: Deseret Book Co., 1958.

Smith, Joseph Fielding. *Doctrines of Salvation.* Salt Lake City: Bookcraft, 1954.

Snow, Lorenzo. *Improvement Era*, June, 1919. Quoted in Daniel H. Ludlow. *Latter-Day Prophets Speak.* n.p.: Daniel H. Ludlow, 1948.

Swartzell, William. *Mormonism Exposed, Being a Journal of a Residence in Missouri from the 28th of May to the 28th of August.* Pekin, Ohio: By the author, 1838.

Talmage, James E. *A Study of the Articles of Faith.* Missionary Reference Set Edition. Salt Lake City: Deseret Book Co., 1983.

Tanner, Jerald and Sandra. *Mormonism—Shadow or Reality?* Salt Lake City: Modern Microfilm Co, 1972.

Times and Seasons. Vols. I-VI. Nauvoo, Illinois, July 1839-February 15, 1846.

Tucker, Pomeroy. *The Origin, Rise and Progress of Mormonism.* New York: D. Appleton & Co, 1867.

Unger, Merrill. *Archaeology and the Old Testament.* Chicago: Moody Press, 1954.

Vine, W.E. *Expository Dictionary of New Testament Words*. Old Tappan,
    New Jersey: Fleming H. Revell Co., 1966.

Walters, Wesley P. *Joseph Smith Among the Egyptians*. Salt Lake City:
    Utah Lighthouse Ministry, 1973, reprinted by permission from *The
    Journal of the Evangelical Theological Society*, Vol. 16, No. 1 (Win-
    ter, 1973).

_____. *New Light on Mormon Origins from the Palmyra (N.Y.)
    Revival*. La Mesa, California: Utah Christian Tract Society, 1973.

Whitmer, David. *An Address to All Believers in Christ*. Richmond, Mis-
    souri: By the author, 1887.

Wilson, John A. *Signs and Wonders upon Pharaoh*. Chicago and Lon-
    don: University of Chicago Press, 1964.

Wood, Bryant G. "Did the Israelites Conquer Jericho? A New Look at the
    Archaeological Evidence." *Biblical Archaeological Review*. Vol. 16,
    No. 2 (March/April, 1990).

Wright, G. Ernest. *Biblical Archaeology*. Philadelphia: The Westminster
    Press, 1960.